Fit Money

MARTIN O'TOOLE

ISBN: 979-8-577-77793-7

To my family

CONTENTS

INTRODUCTION

FINANCIAL FREEDOM THE FIT
MONEY WAY

I have to admit from the outset that I am an unusual accountant. Although I have the qualification, have worked as a CFO for one of the world's top companies, lectured for a world class third level institution and consulted with businesses of many different sizes I have always been fascinated more by people than money.

A number of years ago, I started to give courses to help people manage their money after some of my clients experienced financial difficulties. This led to the development of an eight week program called the Fit Money Plan which has had a positive impact on many participants' lives. I hope what follows does justice to the knowledge I have gained and enhances yours.

The education process normally starts with me being given the opportunity to speak to a large group in a seminar format on the key concepts behind good money management and provide an overview of the course which I have developed to support these. I then run an eight week course for those people who attended the initial seminar and are interested in turning the concepts into skills. This book is written in a "fly on the wall format" as if the reader is actually observing a seminar in January and the following eight weekly classes of the course. Where necessary extra information is provided in italics in an effort to set the scene and bridge the gap between actual attendance and reading.

THE SEMINAR

It was a wet Tuesday evening in January and 50 people had braved the elements to find their path to financial freedom. Given the faith already shown in me I felt a little under pressure to make sure everyone would gain significantly from the night but reassured myself that the message was simple and my job was just to share what I had learned from having a unique insight into other peoples' finances over the years.

I started the seminar with a little exercise to get everyone engaged. I asked each person to hold up their right hand and then look at the hand of the person beside them for 30 seconds. There was a little reluctance, but half a minute silence meant even the stragglers participated. When everyone relaxed again, I asked what the purpose of the activity was and had several responses ranging from a new form of meditation to the development of muscle tone. Perhaps the exercise could be used for these purposes but in this case it was to demonstrate that for the most part everyone's hands are the same and no amount of money would change that. Having agreed that this was the case I asked the class if there were other similarities between humans and we concluded that we are all very alike.

I then went on to build on this concept with the class in the following manner

"So if we are all fundamentally the same how is it that some people seem to be good at managing money and others are always under pressure? Normally I get immediate feedback from class participants that the answer is simple… it's all down to income. If you have enough its easy manage it. But can it really be down to income with large proportions of the population carrying debt?

Take the Household Debt Report for the House of Commons issued in December 2018 which revealed that over half UK adults held unsecured household debt (excluding mortgages) and that 8% of the adult population had not paid bills or debt repayments in 3 of the prior 6 months. This was supported by the findings of a Yougov survey which indicated that more than 8 million people would not be able to pay their rent or mortgage for more than one month from their savings.

Initially I had also believed that income was the key factor as to whether or not money pressures would arise. However I had a lightbulb moment one day which ultimately contradicted this thinking and led me down the path of helping people achieve financial freedom.

It all started from two different client meetings on the same day. I was just finishing up the review of annual accounts with a highly successful professional couple in a very affluent area. They had a considerable income for the year in question which was reflected in the tax liability due. When they told me they wouldn't have the money to pay the tax and actually didn't know if they had enough personal funds at their disposal to get to the end of the month I was flabbergasted. To put this in context there was a Jaguar and Mercedes parked outside and their house was worth several million.

The gravity of the situation was highlighted even more by the fact that earlier that day I had met a couple of much more modest income in their comfortable suburban home and yet they were talking about plans for retiring early when their children finished college due to their mortgage being recently paid off.

So from that day I started to look at clients in a different way and began to research what made the difference between those who were good at managing money and not. Initially I looked into intelligence or if completing relevant degrees in finance made the difference, but this didn't highlight anything significant. I then moved on to looking at those who had gotten all the breaks in life, coming from strong backgrounds, never wanting for anything, to see if that was the differentiator in being good with money but that didn't show anything either. Ultimately the research revealed that no matter what the background, it was behaviour with money that made all the difference. Now it's a simple phrase but not that easy to put in place as lots of people fail to have good behaviour with money.

To try and understand this I started to look at what drives behaviour. What are the influences on our behaviour with money? Because at a basic level it's simply a means to exchange goods and services."

To demonstrate this I asked for a volunteer with £20 promising that they would get it back and there would be no embarrassment. Now it can be hard enough to get volunteers at any time but throw money into the mix and it becomes painful. Thankfully after what seemed like an age Jenny who was in her early thirties and politely confident, stepped forward.

I handed Jenny a block of wood and asked her to place it on the desk with her £20 sitting on top of it. So far so good. I then handed Jenny a hammer and asked her to strike the £20 which was sitting on the block of wood in front of her. Jenny barely tipped the note so I asked her to hit it harder and the second strike had some more force. I then asked Jenny to give the £20 a very hard strike. At this stage the class were all cheering Jenny on and she gave the note a thunderous bang to loud applause. We then inspected the note and agreed it had no damage so there was no replacement needed. As Jenny was about to hand me back the hammer I asked her to do me one more little favour which was to place her lovely hand on the block of wood and strike it with the same force. Jenny looked at me with a very confused face and obviously refused, so I pleaded a little in a funny way to great laughter from the class. Of course Jenny responded that she didn't mind potentially damaging a £20 note but wasn't about to hurt her hand. I thanked Jenny for her help and asked her to return to her seat.

I then outlined that the purpose of the exercise was to show that money is not part of us. To be successful with money and make rational decisions we need to depersonalise our relationship with money. Take the view that its simply a tool, not as important as Jenny's health or anyone's health for that matter.

"So if it's only a tool why would we talk about behaviour with money? Well the truth is that to many people it's much more than a tool. Money and the material items which it buys appears to have become the defining characteristic of success in many people's eyes. So much so that a large percentage of the population will go into debt in order to be able to create an outward image of material success as they feel they are being judged by others on this basis. What's really interesting is that the research shows how we behave as people and the relationships we develop is what really matters rather than what we have accumulated from a material perspective.

The Harvard Study of Adult Development is one of the most defining pieces of work in this area. It has been running for nearly 80 years and is unique in gathering a deep insight into 268 Harvard graduates from the classes of 1939-1944 and a group of 456 people who grew up in the inner-city neighbourhoods of Boston around that time. Professor Waldinger, the current director of the project provides a superb overview of the study in a 2015 Ted talk where he outlines the process of following up with each person on an annual basis to ask about their work, home lives and health. They not only received questionnaires, Waldinger said, but they were also interviewed in their homes, provided their medical records from their doctors, got their blood drawn, their brains scanned and let the researchers talk to their children. After gaining tens of thousands of pages of research data based on these participants, Waldinger outlined that the clearest message from the study was that good relationships are the key to keeping us happier and healthier. I guess we all probably realise this at a deeper level but why then are so many people caught up with thinking that the accumulation of money and material items is what we need to be happy?

Well the reason is "They" want us to!!

But who are "They"????

Well if we take the main elements of a family spend we can see that it's made up of mortgage, cars, food and clothing. Can we broadly say that this money is spent with big banks, big car companies and big retailers? I think we can and it's no secret that the principal goal of these corporations is to make money. After all capitalism is widely understood and the definition is only a click away. The Oxford English dictionary defines it as "An economic and political system in which a country's trade and industry are controlled by private owners for profit."

But we often forget this as corporations spend billions every year advertising and marketing how their products will help us feel happy and fulfilled. Unfortunately there is no one on our side advising whether or not this will be the case, so we accept their story. The only problem being if we believe a product or service is key to our happiness it moves from being a "Want" to a "Need" and we are much more likely to buy it.

These big corporations don't screen each customer to see if they actually "Need" their product or if they can afford it, why would they? Can you imagine the salesperson sitting "Mary" down to see if she really "Needs" the home cinema system or if it suits her budget? In fact, the opposite is often true. Advertising very often tries to convince the potential purchaser that their "Wants" are their "Needs".

You may be thinking that marketing and advertising won't distort your view but be careful as it's very focused and has been convincing customers for a very long time. A little history lesson tells us that in 1920 Ed Bernays who is considered to be the founder of public relations came up with the idea that if marketing was to focus on peoples subconscious and convince them that their "Wants" are their "Needs" business would boom by providing matching products."

I then looked for a volunteer for the next exercise to help turn the theory into reality. John stepped forward, the ideal candidate in being 6ft 2", 26 years of age and ready to rule the world. I firstly asked him if he would eat some grass I had cut from the lawn earlier. An unusual request I know but I outlined that it would make him feel liberated and free. John sensibly declined. I then asked if John would put on a bell bottom jeans I had brought along, outlining that they would make him feel young and cool. Again, John declined suggesting that the clothes wouldn't suit.

Thanking John and releasing him to sit down I then used the exercise to help explain to the class the decision-making process. (Obviously the volunteering hadn't been too traumatic as both John and Jenny signed up for the 8 week course later that evening.)

"We can see that John is making rational decisions on the basis of no advertising. Yet it could be argued that when Ed Bernes used advertising to convince people that cigarettes would make them feel liberated and free they made irrational decisions in relation to their health.

In a similar vein John seems to think that the bell bottom jeans are unusual yet people wear all sorts of clothing when its in fashion. Again, you might be surprised to know that Ed Bernes used advertising to introduce the concept of changes in fashion to help increase sales of clothing. He moved clothing from being functional to an expression of self.

So the net of this history lesson is that corporations very often market in a way that supports irrational decision making in order to boost their profits.

So what about today, with so much information at our fingertips surely we are not making irrational spending decisions? Well I am not sure.

Think of all the things we consider necessities today that a few years ago were considered luxuries. For example, smart phone, latte, convenience meals, wifi, pay per view TV, the list goes on. Sometimes emotional appeals are used to create needs by insinuating that the purchase will make us happy, give us more status, make us more secure etc. Think about the subconscious message in the naming of the BMW 5 Series "Executive Class" of car. Is it that aspiring executives should drive such a car or perhaps you will feel like an executive if you drive one? There is no doubt cars are appealing but how different are they? Is the advertising appealing to our "Wants" or our "Needs"?

An interesting exercise is to use one of the car compare sites to assess a BMW 5 series against a Volkswagen Passat. Broadly speaking they have nearly the same width, height and length but for nearly double the price the BMW will get to 60mph 2.9 seconds faster. £25,000 really is a lot for 2.9 seconds. I wonder how to consciously rationalise that decision.

What about Red Bull advertising? One of their most famous lines is "the only limit is the one you set yourself" and this is supported by images of Felix Baumgartner carrying out a space jump, skydiving an estimated 39km. Now there is no doubt that this was an amazing feat but at a conscious level bears very little relationship to a caffeine and sugar based energy drink. Instead the marketing is aimed at the subconscious to create the link that you will be exciting and adventurous if you drink Red Bull. It is undisputed that Redbull is now the largest energy drink supplier in the world but perhaps their greatest achievement is in marketing.

The good news is the game isn't over. By understanding the rules the corporations play by we can adapt our approach. Think about it, they very often "Need" our money more than we "Need" to spend it. I am emphasising the word need as it's the key to success. If we take a big step back when we are thinking of spending our money and decide what "Need" is being satisfied we are more likely to make wise decisions. If we consciously spend our money on "Needs" rather than "Wants" we will win the game.

So what's a "Need"? Shoes are a "Need", think about it for a second. Close your eyes and imagine walking down the street without shoes in the middle of winter. Think about the pain of the cold and wet on your feet, just like the first step into the sea. Yes, I think we can say shoes are a "Need".

So lets build on that concept, what would you swap for your shoes? Would you give them up for a latte? Probably not. Would you give them up for food? Possibly if you hadn't eaten in a day. Would you give them up for pay per view TV? Probably not. It's surprising, when we take a step back we can actually distinguish between "Wants" and "Needs".

If we do this the purchasing decision becomes so much easier. So let's say armed with our new knowledge we are being presented with a "Want" such as a top of the range TV. We can now make an assessment of what "Need" will be put on the long finger to enable the purchase. Will we put off some mortgage payment and ultimately pay extra interest on the property? If we put £2,000 for the TV on to a 30 year mortgage it could end up costing nearly £4,000. Would we put off paying pension because we believe we will never get old? It seems many people do as a survey by the Financial Conduct Authority in 2017 revealed that 15 million people in the UK have no private pension.

I "Need" help I hear you say, well don't worry its at hand and is called the "Fit Money Plan". Over an 8 week period we will look at how to take control of money to set a path to Financial Freedom. So how do we take control of our money?

We need to get to the point where we understand that money is actually a tool which we use in our lives in order to get the maximum value out of it. But managing money is like running a 5 mile challenge. Some think they can succeed without training but most of these drop out due to exhaustion.

As Benjamin Franklin famously said "Failing to plan is planning to fail". So if we want to successfully run 5 miles we must create a fitness plan. In a similar fashion if we want to successfully manage money we must create a money fitness plan. Just as we train our bodies to get fit we need to train our money to get it fit. And that's what we have created, a simple straight forward Fit Money Plan.

A 5 mile training plan would probably start with exercise in the form of a workout a few days a week. In a similar fashion we have created a money workout. At its core is the creation of a spending plan and tracking expenditure against this so every £1 works harder for you.

There is no quick fix though you must do the workouts. At times it's painful putting on the running gear to go out in the rain, at least with the money workout you can sit at a desk with a coffee. After a few weeks the training for the 5 mile challenge gets a little easier and you don't puff quite as much after workouts. In a similar fashion after a few weeks of the money workouts putting some money aside doesn't take as much effort as before.

The next stage of the 5 mile training plan might be to go for a health check to decide if you are ready to go to the next level, perhaps use your new found fitness to participate in a 2 mile run. In a similar fashion under our Fit Money Plan we carry out a money health check to understand your financial wellbeing.

This involves looking at the progress you have been making with your workouts in the form of savings made or debts reduced. Sometimes a couple of extra training sessions focusing on areas for improvement make all the difference. Follow the fitness plan and the results will come. On the other hand we all know step skipping results in pulled muscles and in the money world credit card debt."

We never discuss anyone's total financial position as participants vary from the wealthy to those with current financial concerns but all share the common goal of learning how to get the most out of their money. The fit money plan is the same no matter what the financial circumstances.

"The next stage of the 5 mile training plan could be to build up endurance through strategic (longer) workouts focusing on the medium-term goal. Setting a plan for the medium term and achieving milestones along the way gives great confidence that you are on the winning path.

You meet others on your training run and give them the smiling wave happy in the knowledge that you are now part of the fit club. In a similar fashion under the fit money plan you move from paying off debts to establishing financial endurance by building up a future investment fund and taking out appropriate insurance. It takes determination though, the person who got to the top of the mountain didn't just drop there.

This may all seem like common sense but unfortunately it's not so common when we look at the results of Life Search's 2017 Health, Wealth and Happiness report which outlined that 60% of the UK adult population haven't taken out life insurance. Take a minute, how would your family fair out if you suddenly passed away? Whatever about hoping to avoid sudden death we can be sure that a rainy day fund won't go to waste because sooner or later it always rains.

The final stage is actually reaping the fruits of your training. Obviously all the workouts make the 5 mile challenge easier but the real benefit is the life changing future options your fitness provides. Perhaps you will run a marathon, climb a mountain or better again take on a significant challenge to raise money for charity. In a similar fashion learning how to be in control of your finances through the Fit Money Plan could be life changing in that it creates lots of future options. Perhaps you pay off your mortgage early, invest to create wealth, retire early and maybe help those you know in need.

You might even discover, to quote Red Bull "the only limit is the one you set yourself".

I normally finish up the seminar with a question and answer session and ask those that might be interested in attending the 8 week course to wait for a few minutes so that I can share some more details of times and dates etc.

CREATE A BUDGET AND BANK ACCOUNT

Another Tuesday in January and I found myself in front of familiar faces eagerly seeking the path to Financial Freedom. About 25 people from the 50 who had attended the initial seminar had made the brave decision to sign up for the course. A reasonable return given the time of year, the many commitments people have to manage and the fact that some will always just hope that things will change without taking any action. But as Einstein famously said "Doing the same thing over and over again and expecting different results is the definition of insanity".

I started by describing that the aim of the course was to help people make informed decisions with their time and money. To do this we would demystify how to be successful in using money to meet our real needs. One of the key elements would be to depersonalise our relationship with spending in order to be able to take a considered approach and make rational decisions.

"Over the next 8 classes we will provide guidance and tools to help you work on your personal finances – the gym equipment if you like. We want to get to the stage where a considered view is taken when making decisions about money.

Many years ago I met a very nice Devon farmer John and his wife Elizabeth on holidays who demonstrated this considered view and I would like to share it with you. We ran into them in the pub one evening while having dinner with our respective families. The kids started playing together and it wasn't long before the parents were chatting and for a brief few minutes felt like individuals again. In any event we clicked and they proceeded to tell us about their lives. Married with three kids they were busy between school drops, homework and children's sports not to mention having to generate an income. Overall they seemed to have a good life and enjoyed family time with a glass of wine on the weekend and even getting to do things as a couple from time to time.

John took great pride in talking about his farm and the joy he got out of building up the dairy herd and Elizabeth was really excited about her new cheese making project. It had started as a small initiative to get some extra income through a cheese stall in the local farmer's market but they had won some prestigious awards and large number of shops were now interested in stocking their products. As luck would have it one of my clients in a different food category had previously brought in investors to turn their small niche business into something much more significant and had made a lot of money. Suffice to say she now drives a Porsche and has two holiday homes.

It's always wonderful to discover a budding successful business and fuelled by the relaxed atmosphere I got very enthusiastic about how using a similar growth model my new-found friends could become wealthy. I outlined some of the grants available for developing rural business and how I had some clients that are always looking for a good investment.

I could easily create a business plan, help get the money on board, have a friend help with the marketing, another with connections in some of the big stores... you get the idea - lots of passion for progress. Anyway, Elizabeth let me finish and explained that it sounded like a great option but she had a few questions. I said "sure" and Elizabeth asked how much money would they need to borrow. I outlined a couple of million at least if she wanted to have an efficient production facility that would meet the required health standards. But we would run production 24x7 to speed up the repayment on the loan. John then asked if they would need staff to run this facility and I outlined that most probably yes. Elizabeth then asked if she would need to be very involved from a day to day perspective. I explained that when investors give you money that they really want you to be 100% committed and if production was going to be 24x7 that would basically mean be on call at all times.

The smile had gone from their faces at this stage. I tried to reengage John and Elizabeth by outlining the millions that my client had made and she was now looking to retire early to spend more time with her family, on projects she enjoys and do some travelling. Elizabeth wondered how long it took my client to make her millions. I responded that it was close to 10 years but at 55 years of age she still had plenty of time to enjoy it. Elizabeth sat back for a minute and said "I am afraid its not for me".

It was a bit of a let-down as I thought I could really help them. When I asked why, Elizabeth outlined that she currently gets to spend lots of time with her family, work on projects she really likes and has a holiday abroad each year. She didn't see the logic in parking her life for 10 years just to live like today but with the addition of a fancy car and holiday homes.

Elizabeth went on to say that in 10 years the kids would be grown up and left the house so spending more time with them would be difficult not to mention there is no guarantee on health. And that my friends was a fundamental lesson in what wealth really is.

I had spent years helping companies and individuals increase their wealth but always from a money perspective, John and Elizabeth had now considered the opportunity in the context of their daily lives and placed a bigger value on time. Perhaps time is the only real currency.

So how can you take back control of your life and have the money you need? Well, as mentioned in Chapter 1 (The Seminar) if we want to successfully run 5 miles we must create a fitness plan. In a similar fashion if we want to successfully manage money we must create a money fitness plan. Just as we train our bodies to get fit we need to train our money to get it fit.

Firstly though congratulations. The fact that you are here (or reading this) puts you ahead of about 70% of the population who have their fingers crossed when going to the ATM at the end of the month without ever looking at the alternative. The following chart illustrates the breakdown of the eight classes of the plan as discussed previously.

5 Mile Fitness Plan	£5k Fit Money Plan	
Workout	Fit Money - Workout	
	W1	Create a Plan
	W2	Input Spending
	W3	Spending Actual v Plan
Health Check	Fit Money- Health Check	
	W4	Asset Review
	W5	Debt Reduction
Endurance Training	Fit Money- Endurance Training	
	W6	Mortgage Review
	W7	Insurance & Pension
Future Options	Fit Money - Future Options	
	W8	Investments

The first step is to create a spending plan for the next year. Consider yourself the financial controller of your household and the idea is you plan more to stress less. Consciously decide how every pound is going to be put to good use. If you want to invest more, save for a rainy day or pay down debt you will need to identify where the funds are going to come from in advance. The creation of the plan often identifies opportunities for using money wisely. Some people say. "Lets track our spending to avoid trouble" but that's like closing the stable door after the horse has bolted. To show you how to do this I have created an example for household spending using the Fit Money Workout Template.

Fit Money Workout Template

		Annual Plan
Salary allocated to Household		57,200
Use of Funds	**Category**	
School Transport	Regular	884
Movies	Regular	0
Electric	Regular	1,612
Gas	Regular	0
Child Minder	Regular	0
Maintenance	Regular	0
Mortgage or Rent	Regular	9,308
Online/Internet Service	Regular	0
Phone (Cellular)	Regular	520
Phone (Home) Broadband	Regular	520
Supplies	Regular	0
Personal	Regular	0
Car Loan	Regular	3,484
Hair/Nails	Regular	2,080
Takeaway Food	Regular	520
Bus/Taxi fare	Regular	0
Fuel	Regular	1,560
Parking fees	Regular	0
Music (CDs, downloads, etc.)	Regular	0
Sporting Events	Regular	0
Dining Out	Regular	1,300
Groceries	Regular	10,400

Christmas Gifts & Entertainment	Irregular	1,560
Holidays	Irregular	2,708
Natural gas/oil	Irregular	2,708
Waste Removal	Irregular	338
Water and Sewer-	Irregular	325
Health Insurance Family	Irregular	1,781
Home Insurance	Irregular	758
Clothing Kids	Irregular	975
School Books	Irregular	325
School Clothes	Irregular	936
Christmas	Irregular	624
Sports Club	Irregular	0
Clothing Adults	Irregular	3,120
Extracurricular activities Kids	Irregular	0
Medical Family	Irregular	650
Dentist	Irregular	130
Medical Pets	Irregular	325
Holidays Pets - Kennel	Irregular	260
Repairs house	Irregular	0
Furniture	Irregular	0
Rates	Irregular	867
Insurance	Irregular	520
Repairs	Irregular	390
Maintenance	Irregular	520
Summary Totals - Spending		
Debit Card Payments for Regular Expenses		32,188
Debit Card Payments for Irregular Expenses		19,812
Summary Totals - Funds left in Bank Account		
Funds for Future Investment- Transfer to Deposit A/C		5,200

There are lots of numbers but don't be scared it's really very straightforward. We read the chart from left to right with the top section being the source of funds representing the planned salary allocated to run the household from an annual perspective. You will note that we talk about salary allocated to run the household which is in keeping with our philosophy of not seeking or disclosing anyone's total financial position. Beneath this we can see how the money is used from an annual perspective.

The second column describes the spending as regular (occurring weekly or monthly) and irregular which means less frequently. This differentiation is half the solution to managing money effectively, the reason being that most people only think of the items which they constantly spend money on but neglect to put funds aside for those expenditures which occur a couple of times a year.

The money spent on irregular items surprises many people and its often hard to believe how much spending falls into this category until you have completed the exercise. In our example irregular expenditure represents over 38% of the planned annual household spending. ie 19,812/52,000.

Now I know we can debate some of the items, but we all know a lot of our spending happens in this way and if we haven't budgeted for irregular expenditure our planning will have gone to waste.

So for next week we are asking each of you to do a little homework. Firstly set up a Fit Money bank account or clear out an existing bank account that you can use to manage your household going forward. Create automatic transfers into the account for the amount you wish to allocate running your household and direct debits out of it for your standard outgoings.

Before you start telling me that you can manage to implement our guidance across the 5 bank accounts you have, let me tell you that there is a huge body of research that says that we are more likely to succeed with specific goals that are easily measured. I can guarantee you its easier manage expenditure from one central location.

Secondly prepare your household spending plan for the year using the Fit Money Workout Template with particular focus on including Regular and Irregular spending. Now enough of the numbers. Who likes running in the dark on their own? Very few I bet! But yet I see groups of happy people running together on my drive home every evening. When I ask my friends who participate in such activities to explain this madness they say it's great being part of a group. They often quote Aristotle who said "The whole is greater than the sum of the individual effort's."

So given that you have all signed up for the next 8 weeks lets work through the Fit Money Plan together to gain from the group dynamic. We will share progress and talk about opportunities and challenges but never disclose anyone's total financial situation. In fact, you could have a million or owe a million and your fellow participants would be none the wiser. Next week I will go through any questions you have one to one. While I am carrying out that exercise I will ask that you chat amongst yourselves about your experience of preparing the annual plan for salary allocation and spending. Really outlining what you found easy or difficult and if you gained any surprising insights. Finally you will be asked to chat about one initiative for maximising your money. As time goes by most people find that their new approach to money management simply reveals opportunities on a daily basis but a little research may be needed for the first couple of weeks. Initiatives can range from the new deals at a discounter store to tax efficient tracker funds. All knowledge is learning, and all learning is good.

Finally for a bit of fun we have our steps to Fit Money Plan and for once its not really what it says on the tin. Subconsciously I had this idea that physical health could be linked to financial health. With this in mind I carried out some research and as you might expect found volumes to show that poor financial health causes stress and physical health issues, but I wondered if it could also work the other way. Ie good physical health could improve finances. Whilst information was limited some research by Washington University showed that people taking an active interest in their physical health are much more likely to make good financial decisions.

So armed with this knowledge I asked some early participants in the course if they would be interested in creating their own steps programme. The team set the challenge which was typically 10,000 steps per day per individual to be tracked on their phones and results shared on a weekly basis.

Surprisingly most people take on the challenge and whilst it hasn't been possible to measure how much progress in money management is down to taking extra exercise, I have no doubt it's a significant help. In any event people love this aspect of the plan so much so that they often walk as a group after the weekly meeting. If you would like to create your own steps to fit money challenge, I am happy to facilitate a fun discussion each week whilst we get everyone's feedback on reaching the agreed number of steps. Why not get a double bonus, improve your financial health and physical health at the same time?"

CLASS TWO

TRACK SPENDING

So here I was back again for another Tuesday with our team. I always love this stage of the plan as even the initial step of creating a spending plan very often has a dramatic effect on the participants. Talk about lightbulb moments! People often move in the space of a week from having their heads in the sand on money matters to being able to quote cost per kilowatt of the various electrical suppliers. Given the size of the class I had people email me their Fit Money Workout Template in advance of the session and had a brief one on one chat with a couple of participants who had struggled putting their spending plans together. All the while the group were having a discussion about their experience of sitting down and working out how they use money and creating their projections for moving forward on the Fit Money Workout Template. Essentially outlining what was easy or difficult and any surprising insights gained. Here is some of their feedback.

Mary – a young solicitor with an image to keep and a young family….

"I couldn't believe that nearly half our spending fitted

into the irregular category arising only a couple of times a year but often requiring significant funds. For the first time ever I realised how we go from having a reasonable balance in the bank one month to practically nothing the following month."

John – single self-employed electrician with a new BMW

"I think I must have made a mistake with putting the numbers together because it looks like I will have very little left after a few nights out a week and keeping a car on the road. How can this be when I earn more than most of my buddies? Surely you have to be able to afford decent clothes and a social life when working?"

Jenny- accountant living at home with parents and working with a global company

"I enjoyed putting the numbers together, it was good to see that I can afford to eat in nice restaurants and use taxis whenever I want. My mum is always telling me that I waste my money but thankfully I can now show her how I can save a little on a weekly basis."

Liam – middle aged Civil Servant with teenage children and older parents

"I didn't get to complete the exercise as I had a very stressful week ferrying the kids around to activities and spent the weekend looking after my parents. When I sat down on Sunday night to put the details into the template, I was exhausted and needed a glass of wine to maintain my sanity."

The rules of the plan are that participants are not allowed comment negatively on the other participants inputs as it's a journey of self-discovery and the more others share the more we discover about ourselves.

From my perspective I am just trying to get a picture of each person's relationship with money at this stage. I offered very little feedback except to mention to Liam that I would help him put his template together as controlling finances would certainly reduce some of the stress in his life. I then wanted to get the participants really focused on the next stage which tracks actual spending and as it involves some work I knew I needed to create some extra motivation. I did this by questioning why more people don't have the wisdom of the Devon farmers.

"You will remember we chatted last week about John and Elizabeth the Devon farmers. Well on returning from holiday I had their ethos for about a month and then seemed to fall back into my usual routine without realising it. From time to time I would remember their story and make a little effort to smell the flowers more, but it never lasted very long.

This started to bug me, so I carried out a little research and realised that John and Elizabeth were not the first people to place a value on time. In fact, as far back as 1930 the famous economist John Maynard Keynes had a wonderful vision in that he predicted as economies developed the working week would be drastically cut, to perhaps 15 hours a week. He thought people would choose to have far more leisure as their needs were satisfied. Keynes suggested people in 2030 would be eight times better off than people in the 1930's and parents would spend more time with their children.

We all know that the reality is something different. In her book "Willing Slaves" Madeline Bunting outlines that modern thinking seduces millions of people to hand over the best part of their lives to their employer. Physical hardships of working in old mills have been replaced by new psychological hardships of trying to achieve wealth in monetary terms.

In "The Overworked American" Juliet Schor tells us that the average American works one month more per year today than in 1970. A Harvard business survey of 1000 people discovered 94% worked more than 50 hours per week and 50% worked in excess of 65 hours. So how has this happened you might ask? Well it's not a law of nature, actually the answer can be found in what we discussed in the opening seminar. We live and work in a capitalist, economic and political system in which a country's trade and industry are controlled by private owners for profit.

Therefore, the truth lies in a simple equation;

Profit = Sales − Cost of Sales

So to grow profits corporations must increase sales and reduce costs.

To increase sales corporations, spend billions every year advertising and marketing how their products will help us feel happy and fulfilled. Remember Ed Bernes working with the tobacco and garment industries? That was only the start.

To put this into perspective we need only look at global advertising spending increasing from $100 billion in 1980 to over $600 billion in 2019 (World Advertising and Research Center (WARC)/CNN), with the result that the average person gets the equivalent of a year's marketing in 1960 in just one week today.

Let's look at some practical examples of how this boosts company sales. If the employee buys the earlier mentioned BMW Executive Car at £40k rather than the average car at £20k it creates 100% more income for the seller. If the employee takes out a mortgage at £250k rather than £150k it creates £100k more income for the chain. ie Developer, Builder, Government, Local Authority, Auctioneer, Solicitor, Bank. If the amount borrowed increases by £100k it creates nearly £100k more interest for the bank. A lot of people benefit if we pay more money for our houses. But we will come back to that later.

To reduce costs, corporations need to get more productivity from their employees. This has largely been achieved through non-confrontational methods such as giving an employee an increase in salary and promoting them to a "higher grade" but creating the expectation that they will work unpaid overtime.

Now before you decide to blame all the worlds ills on the big corporations take a step back for a moment. None of this is a secret...remember the definition of capitalism. "An economic and political system in which a country's trade and industry are controlled by private owners for profit".

It could be argued that the corporations are as much a victim as the employees given they are constantly under pressure to achieve short-term profits for their shareholders. In fact, it's a much stronger argument than you might think. Michael Dell spent nearly $5 billion of his own money taking Dell Computers private in 2013 to enable decision making to be based on a longer-term view without fear of dramatic fall in the company share price. But who are these shareholders? Well guess what? Its you and me... and why do we push so hard for good short-term investment returns? Because we have a lot of "Wants" to satisfy and require extra money to do so. Lets not focus on others, rather look in the mirror and ask ourselves if extra money is really required to meet our actual "Needs"? But how can we focus on this in todays world I hear you say? Start thinking about shoes! If a desired purchase is more important than having a pair of shoes then its most likely a "Need".

So armed with all this knowledge what can we do to move forward? Well the answer is to create our own little formula focused on what's important to us as follows;

Salary Allocated to Household – Spend on "Needs" = Fit Money Investment Fund.

You have already created an annual spending plan. Would this now change if we looked at the funds required to meet our budgeted "Needs"? If we went through the initial list of planned spending and eliminated some "Wants", would it create excess funds which could be put to better use? Looking at our example perhaps £2,184 for Christmas spending is over and above what could be set aside to cover reasonable needs? What about £2,080 on Hair & Nails? Imagine if we could half both these expenditure, it would free up an additional £2,132.

What about car repayments? Do we need a new car?

So just as the person who got to the top of the mountain didn't drop there but rather worked step by step, we breakdown the annual money management into a step by step process. You have already completed step one in the preparation of the initial planned use of funds and step two is simply to review this in the context of today's discussion on "Needs".

The next chart shows each item of annual spending divided by 52 to get an estimate of the weekly cost of an item. This is shown in the column weekly plan even if we don't actually pay out money each week.

Fit Money Workout Template		Annual Plan	Weekly Plan
Salary allocated to Household		57,200	1,100
Use of Funds	Category		
School Transport	Regular	884	17
Movies	Regular	0	0
Electric	Regular	1,612	31
Gas	Regular	0	0
Child Minder	Regular	0	0
Maintenance	Regular	0	0
Mortgage or Rent	Regular	9,308	179
Online/Internet Service	Regular	0	0
Phone (Cellular)	Regular	520	10
Phone (Home) Broadband	Regular	520	10
Supplies	Regular	0	0
Personal	Regular	0	0
Car Loan	Regular	3,484	67
Hair/Nails	Regular	2,080	40
Takeaway Food	Regular	520	10
Bus/Taxi fare	Regular	0	0
Fuel	Regular	1,560	30
Parking fees	Regular	0	0
Music (CDs, downloads, etc.)	Regular	0	0
Sporting Events	Regular	0	0
Dining Out	Regular	1,300	25
Groceries	Regular	10,400	200

Christmas Gifts & Entertainment	Irregular	1,560	30
Holidays	Irregular	2,708	52
Natural gas/oil	Irregular	2,708	52
Waste Removal	Irregular	338	7
Water and Sewer-	Irregular	325	6
Health Insurance Family	Irregular	1,781	34
Home Insurance	Irregular	758	15
Clothing Kids	Irregular	975	19
School Books	Irregular	325	6
School Clothes	Irregular	936	18
Christmas	Irregular	624	12
Sports Club	Irregular	0	0
Clothing Adults	Irregular	3,120	60
Extracurricular activities Kids	Irregular	0	0
Medical Family	Irregular	650	13
Dentist	Irregular	130	3
Medical Pets	Irregular	325	6
Holidays Pets - Kennel	Irregular	260	5
Repairs house	Irregular	0	0
Furniture	Irregular	0	0
Rates	Irregular	867	17
Insurance	Irregular	520	10
Repairs	Irregular	390	8
Maintenance	Irregular	520	10
Summary Totals - Spending			
Debit Card Payments for Regular Expenses		32,188	619
Debit Card Payments for Irregular Expenses		19,812	381

Lets take a couple of examples to make sense of this type of approach. The regular spending is reasonably straightforward as we are actually expecting to pay for these needs on a weekly or monthly basis and it makes sense to plan to have funds available to meet these requirements. The irregular spending is more difficult. If we take car insurance as an example we need this every time we drive on a public road but may only be required to pay the premium once per year. Holiday funds are a little more complicated as the costs and benefits are only realised a couple of times a year but if we haven't planned for these on an ongoing basis funds may not be available when required.

As I ask you to start using our Fit Money Templates I am reminded of the faith story where a swimmer gets caught in a riptide whilst in the sea. They get pulled 100 yards from the shore by the tide and a kayaker comes alongside and asks if they are ok. The swimmer outlines that they have faith and will be fine.

About 15 minutes later the swimmer is about 500 yards from the coast and a lifeguard boat comes alongside and asks that they come out of the water. The swimmer outlines that they have faith and will be fine.

About 20 minutes later the swimmer is over a mile from the coast and a rescue helicopter is launched to save them. At this stage the swimmer is really struggling to keep going but when the winchman asks that they put on the safety harness to be lifted into the helicopter they outline that that they have faith and will be fine.

I guess you know what happened next. About 20 minutes later the swimmer drowns and the first question they have on going through the pearly gates is "What am I doing here? I had faith that you would save me." A comforting voice comes from on high and says, "Firstly I sent a kayaker to help and you ignored it. Secondly I sent a life guard and you ignored them. Thirdly I sent a helicopter rescue team and you ignored them. What more could I do when you wouldn't take all the help being offered."

How, you might ask, does this relate to money management templates? Well the answer is that they are performing the same function as the kayaker, lifeboat and helicopter in that they are supports to maintain your financial health. So let's make them work.

The good news is that the next chart showing the Weekly Plan view is prepopulated on your Fit Money Workout Templates using a formula and all you need to do is to look at the column next to Annual Plan for week 1. Each item of annual spending divided by 52 to get an estimate of the weekly cost of an item. This is shown in the column weekly plan even if we don't actually pay out money each week. Having gone through the process of creating our weekly spending plan, the next logical step is to track our weekly spending.

To keep this as simple as possible we suggest that you pay for all your needs in a way that reflects the details of the expenditure on your bank statement. Usually this means direct debits for larger items such as mortgage and using a debit card for payments throughout the week. If you have been on monthly payments for your mortgage move to weekly, this may even save you a lot in interest over time.

On a selected day each week you can then take a printout of your bank statement and fill in the details in the expenditure column on the template. The chart below shows week one planned expenditure and the actual expenditure column populated from bank statement detail.

You will note that the summary section at the bottom of the Fit Money Workout Template brings together all the actual spending on regular expenses for comparison with the planned and likewise with the irregular expenses. So for next week I want you to review your initial budget in light of our discussion tonight and create a spending plan based on "Needs" with a view to reducing spending and building an investment fund on a weekly basis. In addition, I would like you to key in your actual spending for the week into the various categories.

As Warren Buffet famously said, "don't save what is left after spending but spend what is left after savings"

Fit Money Workout Template		Annual Plan	Weekly Plan	Week 1 Actual
Salary allocated to Household		57,200	1,100	1,100
Use of Funds	**Category**			
School Transport	Regular	884	17	15
Movies	Regular	0	0	50
Electric	Regular	1,612	31	0
Gas	Regular	0	0	0
Child Minder	Regular	0	0	0
Maintenance	Regular	0	0	0
Mortgage or Rent	Regular	9,308	179	179
Online/Internet Service	Regular	0	0	0
Phone (Cellular)	Regular	520	10	0
Phone (Home) Broadband	Regular	520	10	0
Supplies	Regular	0	0	0
Personal	Regular	0	0	0
Car Loan	Regular	3,484	67	67
Hair/Nails	Regular	2,080	40	42
Takeaway Food	Regular	520	10	20
Bus/Taxi fare	Regular	0	0	0
Fuel	Regular	1,560	30	79
Parking fees	Regular	0	0	0
Music (CDs, downloads, etc.)	Regular	0	0	0
Sporting Events	Regular	0	0	0
Dining Out	Regular	1,300	25	21
Groceries	Regular	10,400	200	196

Christmas Gifts & Entertainment	**Irregular**	1,560	30	30
Holidays	**Irregular**	2,708	52	
Natural gas/oil	**Irregular**	2,708	52	100
Waste Removal	**Irregular**	338	7	
Water and Sewer-	**Irregular**	325	6	
Health Insurance Family	**Irregular**	1,781	34	0
Home Insurance	**Irregular**	758	15	0
Clothing Kids	**Irregular**	975	19	40
School Books	**Irregular**	325	6	
School Clothes	**Irregular**	936	18	
Christmas	**Irregular**	624	12	0
Sports Club	**Irregular**	0	0	0
Clothing Adults	**Irregular**	3,120	60	20
Extracurricular activities Kids	**Irregular**	0	0	
Medical Family	**Irregular**	650	13	
Dentist	**Irregular**	130	3	
Medical Pets	**Irregular**	325	6	
Holidays Pets - Kennel	**Irregular**	260	5	
Repairs house	**Irregular**	0	0	0
Furniture	**Irregular**	0	0	
Rates	**Irregular**	867	17	50
Insurance	**Irregular**	520	10	
Repairs	**Irregular**	390	8	
Maintenance	**Irregular**	520	10	
Summary Totals - Spending				
Debit Card Payments for Regular Expenses		32,188	619	669
Debit Card Payments for Irregular Expenses		19,812	381	240

"Now tell me about your initiatives and if you have been doing the step challenge."

Mary - the young solicitor with an image to keep and a young family....

"We were on holidays recently and our flight was delayed. We had the children with us and whilst giving the other half the bad news that it was going to cost a fortune to buy a wholesome family meal another passenger overheard us and suggested we keep the receipts that the Airline might cover the cost. I phoned the airline when I returned from holiday and to my great surprise they covered the cost of the meal without any argument."

John - the single self-employed electrician with a new BMW

"I bought a house a couple of years ago and some of the lads were pestering me to rent a room but I always thought it wouldn't be worth the hassle with what I would be left with after tax. That was until I read an article which outlined that I could claim rent a room relief and basically get tax free income for the room. There are limits but if any of you are in a similar position, I would strongly recommend it."

Jenny - the accountant living at home with parents and working with a global company

"I know some people regularly shop in discount stores, but I hadn't and did so last week given I had signed up for the Fit Money course. Well I couldn't believe that they sold award winning wines for under £5. I actually opened a second bottle with my Mum last Friday night."

Liam - the middle aged Civil Servant with teenage

children and older parents

" As I mentioned earlier it was a really bad week for me but I was still looking forward to the course, as apart from learning about how to get ahead with money it offers me a couple of hours away from the stress that seems to be everywhere currently. I suppose I should be honest and say that the step challenge really appealed to me as I never get exercise anymore but I didn't get out to walk. Although in keeping with the spirit of things I got fitted for a good brand of runners in a high-street shop during my lunch break last Friday and went home that evening and bought the runners online for 50% of the recommended retail price."

Fantastic, so you have really done your homework. I will be taking note of each of your initiatives as in truth they could be of great benefit to many people. But what about your step challenge did you have any time left for this given your busy schedules?"

I was surprised to hear that everyone made an effort and while Jenny had completed 90,000 steps in the week by walking instead of taking a bus Mary probably had the most interesting insight. Between work and children Mary was on the go from dawn to dusk and had a constant stress headache but given her diligent nature did not want to attend the course without giving it her best efforts. Ultimately Mary had completed 4,000 steps by walking at lunchtime on Monday to Friday but the breakthrough was the unexpected disappearance of her stress headache and more productive afternoons. John outlined he had been too busy. We finished up for the night and following the tradition established by previous participants the group went for a 30 minute walk.

COMPARE ACTUAL AND PLANNED SPENDING

Class Three is always the toughest as a huge amount of knowledge has been taken on board and the comparison of actual with planned spending has occurred in every household before the meeting. Very often these discussions lead to differences of opinion and so the intention of the session is twofold. Firstly, to re-emphasise that we must depersonalise the decision-making process to be successful and secondly how to analyse the information in the Fit Money Workout template to really get the most out of the money available.

As usual I had a look at the templates in advance and had a conversation with a couple of people who struggled putting the details together while the group chatted about their experiences of putting actual spending into the template. I learned long ago that the best way to draw attention to a weakness or oversight is to ask a question. This generally helps those concerned gain a much greater insight into the situation rather than me simply pointing out areas for improvement and so I adopted the same approach for our opening discussion on the last 7 days.

Mary – a young solicitor with an image to keep and a young family outlined

"It was more complicated to put together my actual spending than I thought it would be. Ultimately my husband and I agreed that we would buy everything using the funds from the Fit Money Bank Account, but he paid for the weekly shopping on his credit card. I then had to transfer funds out of the Fit Money Bank Account to the credit card to have the bank account and the template reflect the true picture."

And I asked

"Would it have saved time if your husband had used the debit card? What other items of expenditure might cause complications from a tracking perspective and how might you incorporate them into your template? Don't answer now but come back next week having thought about it."

John – single self-employed electrician with a new BMW

" With the exception of large items of expenditure such as mortgage or car repayments I have always used cash and it's probably helped keep my spending in check. Say for example I am out with the lads and I have to pay £30 for a round of drinks. Well I will make sure that I only buy when it comes around to my turn again if I have to dig out another £30. I was out last Friday night and found tapping my card made me feel loaded. The only problem being when I checked the account the next day I found that I had left a lot more money in the pub than I normally would."

And I asked

" Did the debit card approach help track other spending? Have a think over the week as to how you might get the information into your template without using the debit card or perhaps using it some of the time? Would that make things easier for you?"

Jenny- accountant living at home with parents and working with a global company

"I have always used my debit card for expenditure and check my statements on a weekly basis, so it was nice to see that the course was recommending this. I did have some difficulty in distinguishing "Wants" from "Needs". Take for example where to eat out on a Saturday night. The girls always like to eat in a Michelin restaurant as a treat for working hard all week. To some extent I can see that this is a little extravagant but on the other had I feel the "Need" to be with my friends."

And I asked

"Remember our discussion about shoes being a "Need"? Using this as a benchmark what effect would it have on your choice of restaurant? No doubt you have a real "Need" to be with your friends but are you passing up on other "Needs" by choice of restaurant? If you had an extra 10, 000 pounds per year in the bank, what would you do? Why not take the week to think about it?"

Liam – middle aged Civil Servant with teenage children and older parents

" I had a row with my wife. When we started looking at the planned spend again it became obvious that the reason we don't save anything is because we both have short-term "Wants" and feel we deserve to live like our neighbours and colleagues. I took the view that we could cut back a fair bit on holidays and Christmas, but only realised afterwards that I neglected to consider that we could be driving a much more cost efficient car than the BMW I had so strongly pushed for when we were changing last year. It all ended up fine as we agreed to track our spending for a while before making any decisions on what to cut back on."

And I asked

"Good that you sorted things out as we don't want to be to blame for family arguments. I wonder if there is any risk with simply tracking spending? Remember our discussion on the horse bolting in the context of expenditure? Have a chat at home over the coming week as to issues that could arise if you simply track spending?"

I then wanted to work with the participants on how to analyse the information which the template was now showing them, although I was pretty sure that they were already comparing actual with planned expenditure. Obviously this would be a good start but to be really effective I need participants to have a complete change in mindset, to depersonalise money and view it as a tool to be managed rather than being managed by it. So I recalled the experiment with the £20 and the hammer on the first night.

"So you all remember the experiment on the first night with £20 and Jenny responded that she didn't mind potentially damaging some money but wasn't about to hurt her hand. We need to remember this as we start to analyse our money, it's not part of us rather it's a tool that we want to get maximum use out of. That's why we are putting it through a training plan to get it as fit as possible so it can deliver maximum value for you. Therefore, the little bit of pain when analysing spending and adopting a new approach with your money is all about the long-term gain.

Now if you are sitting there thinking I have heard all of this before give yourself a pat on the back because you have. If you remember this now, hopefully you will be able to recall the same concept in the future when emotions come to the fore while analysing your money.

The key to success is to depersonalise our relationship with money.

So what about the analysis? Well, it's very simple really if you view the next column on your template you will see that it reveals a comparison of our planned expenditure in the week versus actual. Lets look at our example template from last week to work through the process.

Unusually the best way to read the template is to go to the summary section which is at the bottom first. There we can see that the total of the actual regular expenses of £669 exceeded the plan by £50 and the irregular expenses of £240 coming in £141 in less than plan. We can then understand how we have got to this result by looking at the details in the rows above which compare actual expenditure against plan on a line item basis.

Fit Money Workout Template		Annual Plan	Weekly Plan	Week 1 Actual	Difference
Salary allocated to Household		57,200	1,100	1,100	0
Use of Funds	**Category**				
School Transport	Regular	884	17	15	2
Movies	Regular	0	0	50	-50
Electric	Regular	1,612	31	0	31
Gas	Regular	0	0	0	0
Child Minder	Regular	0	0	0	0
Maintenance	Regular	0	0	0	0
Mortgage or Rent	Regular	9,308	179	179	0
Online/Internet Service	Regular	0	0	0	0
Phone (Cellular)	Regular	520	10	0	10
Phone (Home) Broadband	Regular	520	10	0	10
Supplies	Regular	0	0	0	0
Personal	Regular	0	0	0	0
Car Loan	Regular	3,484	67	67	0
Hair/Nails	Regular	2,080	40	42	-2
Takeaway Food	Regular	520	10	20	-10
Bus/Taxi fare	Regular	0	0	0	0
Fuel	Regular	1,560	30	79	-49
Parking fees	Regular	0	0	0	0
Music (CDs, downloads, etc.)	Regular	0	0	0	0
Sporting Events	Regular	0	0	0	0
Dining Out	Regular	1,300	25	21	4
Groceries	Regular	10,400	200	196	4

Christmas Gifts & Entertainment	Irregular	1,560	30	30	0
Holidays	Irregular	2,708	52		52
Natural gas/oil	Irregular	2,708	52	100	-48
Waste Removal	Irregular	338	7		7
Water and Sewer-	Irregular	325	6		6
Health Insurance Family	Irregular	1,781	34	0	34
Home Insurance	Irregular	758	15	0	15
Clothing Kids	Irregular	975	19	40	-21
School Books	Irregular	325	6		6
School Clothes	Irregular	936	18		18
Christmas	Irregular	624	12	0	12
Sports Club	Irregular	0	0	0	0
Clothing Adults	Irregular	3,120	60	20	40
Extracurricular activities Kids	Irregular	0	0		0
Medical Family	Irregular	650	13		13
Dentist	Irregular	130	3		3
Medical Pets	Irregular	325	6		6
Holidays Pets - Kennel	Irregular	260	5		5
Repairs house	Irregular	0	0	0	0
Furniture	Irregular	0	0		0
Rates	Irregular	867	17	50	-33
Insurance	Irregular	520	10		10
Repairs	Irregular	390	8		8
Maintenance	Irregular	520	10		10
Summary Totals – Spending					
Debit Card Payments for Regular Expenses		32,188	619	669	-50
Debit Card Payments for Irregular Expenses		19,812	381	240	141

For the regular category we can see that the overspend in fuel is being covered by the underspending in electricity and phone charges. However the overspend on movies isn't covered elsewhere and so we end the week £50 overspent and this results in £50 less being set aside for investment.

You may be thinking now what's the point of all of this if I can't go to the movies. Well bingo! You are correct you should be able to go the movies but what will you forgo to satisfy this "Want"? Perhaps the takeaway food could have been skipped for one week. How much of the grocery bill included alcohol intended for a Friday night in, which ended up being a night out? Remember the charts here are just by way of example, it will mean much more to you when looking at your own spending profile.

We would expect the irregular spending to be less than plan given our earlier discussions about car insurance coming up for payment once a year and holiday expenses occurring a couple of times a year. The first option to make the management of this type of expenditure straightforward is to ask the provider if you can pay on a weekly basis. Otherwise we must make sure underspending in the irregular category is ring fenced and set aside for the inevitable effect of timing and available for the once off payment as required.

Continuing with the car insurance example if we had to pay once per year we would expect an underspend of 10 pounds on this line for each week per year with the exception of the week in which the payment is made. We know from the Spending Plan that we will need to have £520 set aside by the time the insurance bill arrives to avoid having to take funds from other categories or borrowing.

Holiday funds are a little more complicated as the costs and benefits are only realised a couple of times a year but if we haven't planned for these on an ongoing basis funds may not be available when required. Again we would expect to see an underspend on these lines outside the holiday period and the key is not to have an overspend in other categories that spoils our fun in the sun.

In the chart below we can see that we didn't use any of our allocated funds for holidays in week 1 which means if everything else went to plan that £52 would have been put aside for holidays in week 1 and form part of the funds left in the bank at the end of the week.

Unfortunately gas and oil are over spent in that we had a spending plan of £52 but actually had to pay out £100. This may simply be due to timing in that we had planned to pay 52 every week but the actual bill from the gas company is biweekly. We will keep an eye on the spending in this category over the coming weeks to ensure it is only a timing issue. If it becomes apparent that the spending plan has been underestimated we will need to cut back spending in other areas to generate the extra amount needed for gas and oil.

This will also apply to a lesser extent to other categories of irregular spending where we will probably have more discretion to cut our cloth to measure if it looks like the expenditure is getting out of control. In the example below we can see that there was an overspend on children's clothing of £21 in week 1. If this trend was to continue for a period of time we could bring our spending back in line with plan by deciding not to buy children's clothing until this occurred.

The full picture can now be seen as we open up the last section of the template to reveal funds which are now left available for future irregular spending and funds for future investment as per below. We can now see that our spending in week 1 when compared to plan reveals that we have £191 left in the account at the end of the week.

£50 has been set aside for Investment and £141 has been set aside for future irregular spending.

Assuming its only timing difference on irregular spending we would be happy with the week but its disappointing that we have £50 less than plan set aside for future investment. We will obviously need the irregular funds set aside to be used when the timing effect is realised. But the funds for future investment should be transferred to a bank deposit account set up specifically for this purpose.

Fit Money Workout Template

		Annual Plan	Weekly Plan	Week 1 Actual	Difference
Salary allocated to Household		57,200	1,100	1,100	0
Use of Funds	**Category**				
School Transport	Regular	884	17	15	2
Movies	Regular	0	0	50	-50
Electric	Regular	1,612	31	0	31
Gas	Regular	0	0	0	0
Child Minder	Regular	0	0	0	0
Maintenance	Regular	0	0	0	0
Mortgage or Rent	Regular	9,308	179	179	0
Online/Internet Service	Regular	0	0	0	0
Phone (Cellular)	Regular	520	10	0	10
Phone (Home) Broadband	Regular	520	10	0	10
Supplies	Regular	0	0	0	0
Personal	Regular	0	0	0	0
Car Loan	Regular	3,484	67	67	0
Hair/Nails	Regular	2,080	40	42	-2
Takeaway Food	Regular	520	10	20	-10
Bus/Taxi fare	Regular	0	0	0	0
Fuel	Regular	1,560	30	79	-49
Parking fees	Regular	0	0	0	0
Music (CDs, downloads, etc.)	Regular	0	0	0	0
Sporting Events	Regular	0	0	0	0
Dining Out	Regular	1,300	25	21	4
Groceries	Regular	10,400	200	196	4

Christmas Gifts & Entertainment	Irregular	1,560	30	30	0
Holidays	Irregular	2,708	52		52
Natural gas/oil	Irregular	2,708	52	100	-48
Waste Removal	Irregular	338	7		7
Water and Sewer-	Irregular	325	6		6
Health Insurance Family	Irregular	1,781	34	0	34
Home Insurance	Irregular	758	15	0	15
Clothing Kids	Irregular	975	19	40	-21
School Books	Irregular	325	6		6
School Clothes	Irregular	936	18		18
Christmas	Irregular	624	12	0	12
Sports Club	Irregular	0	0	0	0
Clothing Adults	Irregular	3,120	60	20	40
Extracurricular activities Kids	Irregular	0	0		0
Medical Family	Irregular	650	13		13
Dentist	Irregular	130	3		3
Medical Pets	Irregular	325	6		6
Holidays Pets – Kennel	Irregular	260	5		5
Repairs house	Irregular	0	0	0	0
Furniture	Irregular	0	0		0
Rates	Irregular	867	17	50	-33
Insurance	Irregular	520	10		10
Repairs	Irregular	390	8		8
Maintenance	Irregular	520	10		10
Total Spending					
Payments for Regular Expenses		32,188	619	669	-50
Payments for Irregular Expenses		19,812	381	240	141
Funds in Bank					
Funds for Future Investment- Transfer to Deposit A/C		5,200	100	50	-50
Funds for Future Irregular expenses			0	141	141

I appreciate that the chart now has a lot of numbers, it reminds me of an episode when I was a junior accountant in practice. At the time I would have received more money in unemployment benefit without having to make tea and photocopy for everyone. With 12 hour days and weekends studying for accountancy exams, we were less than excited when our manager suggested we prepare a 50 page report for each client based on their accounts without exception.

As a diligent junior I prepared a 50 page report from a set of accounts for one client who had a part-time market stall with 10,000 in turnover. You can imagine their surprise when I handed over the 50 pages. There was certainly no extra fees going to be paid. A peer of mine (obeying orders from on high) prepared a 50 page report for a non-trading company only for one of the directors to request that he be sacked for such stupidity. Sense did prevail in the medium term in that it was recognised that information is only useful to a client if firstly it makes sense to them and secondly will be used.

With this in mind the Fit Money analysis is kept as straightforward as possible by only updating one week at a time. Whilst this means the basic template will have more data at each stage, we use the picture paints a thousand words concept (but with numbers) to portray progress in a transparent way on pie charts. Taking the details from the previous page for week 1 plan v actual, they can be very quickly interpreted on the following pie charts, where each slice represents a category of expenditure. Essentially for week 1 we can see that we have set aside less money for future investment than anticipated in the plan but more to irregular expenses.

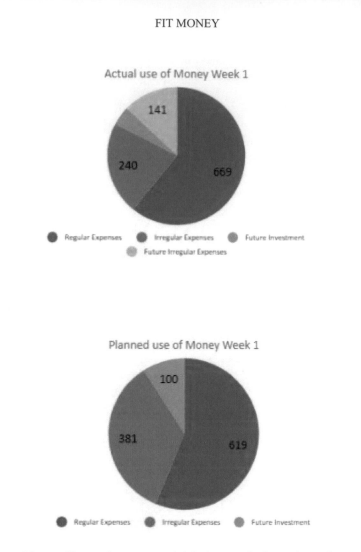

Actual use of Money Week 1

141
240
669

Regular Expenses · Irregular Expenses · Future Investment
Future Irregular Expenses

Planned use of Money Week 1

100
381
619

Regular Expenses · Irregular Expenses · Future Investment

Now tell me about your initiatives and if you have been doing the step challenge.

Mary – the young solicitor with an image to keep and a young family….

"Every year I say to myself that I am going to spend a couple of hours getting different quotes for car insurance as it's really getting out of hand. Anyhow as you probably guessed if I have a choice between a client that needs something quickly or phoning around for quotes, I will always put the client first. But given I am participating in this course I decided that I had better make the effort and after a couple of calls I reduced my bill by 15%. I thought about it afterwards and the truth is that I simply avoided this other years as I didn't want to take on the task. Had I known it would save me hundreds of pounds I would have done it long ago."

John - the single self-employed electrician with a new BMW

" I never bothered with a loyalty card before because to be honest I just picked up groceries when I needed them at whatever shop I was passing. Now since I started the course I have cut down on the takeaways and actually need to do a proper shop each week. Interestingly the main benefit comes when I can use the points to get a pizza so I don't actually have to give up all the fast food."

Jenny - the accountant living at home with parents and working with a global company

"I became a named driver on my parents car a couple of years ago and insisted that I paid the insurance as I don't pay rent or anything like that at home. I was actually surprised it was so expensive and as its coming up for renewal I decided to look for a cheaper option. I was amazed that I could save nearly 25% by using a black box in the car that records my driving and sends the details to the insurance company. Obviously I have to drive within the speed limits but I always drive in line with the law as everyone should."

Liam - the middle-aged Civil Servant with teenage children and older parents

"My wife has been pestering me for years to do

something about the heating in our house. It's a bit of a bone of contention as I grew up in a very old house and if you were cold the answer was to put on a jumper or go for a walk whereas my wife grew up in a well-insulated suburban home. If it was up to me I would be fine but I want my wife to be happy as she is so good to myself and the kids. So I decided that if we could save the money using the course structure, we would put it into upgrading the house. I started to look into this a few days ago and absolutely couldn't believe the grant aid available. It seems that we will probably get huge discounts on a boiler and insulation not to mention the reduction in energy bills. I could kick myself for not looking into this before."

"That's really super feedback, I will be noting these initiatives to share with others. You are even motivating me at this stage. But with all this good work did you get out for some steps?"

Jenny as expected had completed 70,000 steps in the week and took the bus a couple of days to create some time to look into mortgages. On the basis of feeling less stressed from the first weeks walking Mary kept up the lunchtime routine. Liam was the surprise of the week. Having walked at lunch for a few days he decided upon arriving home on Thursday evening to go for a jog. Now, Liam outlined that with the exception of his boxers he hadn't had a pair of shorts on in 15 years! He felt so invigorated after the jog that he managed to keep up the exercise and completed 60,000 steps in the week. John outlined he was very stressed by the time he got home every day and a walk just seemed like torture. That said he did go for a walk after the class with the other participants.

NET ASSET REVIEW

I couldn't believe that this was the fourth class of the Fit Money Plan. The focus of this week was to take the team through the process of how they might prepare an overall view of their financial position. Again sticking with the ethos of not disclosing anyone's wealth I provide a template which enables the preparation of a statement of overall financial position but doesn't require its submission as part of the course. But before getting into the new material I knew there was trouble brewing as John had not submitted his Fit Money Workout Template for the second week in a row. It was surprising really in that John seemed very interested in understanding his finances whilst in the meeting but didn't seem to be carrying that enthusiasm through the week. As usual I asked everyone to have a chat about their experiences over the past 7 days. We would then discuss their findings as a group, focusing on the positives which could be shared. In addition, I outlined that I was going to chat to John about his template for 5 minutes. (knowing that none had been submitted)
. I then went over to a quiet corner with John and explained that his strong personality was a great addition to the course but wondered why he wasn't managing to get the template completed. John outlined that in truth

he liked learning how to manage money and was definitely spending less but didn't see the benefit in going through the effort of sitting down and putting the template together after a long day at work.

I then asked if John's finances were in good shape overall. John outlined that he always had enough and had managed to buy a house albeit with some help from his parents. It's difficult to argue against the logic of avoiding an exercise where the benefits don't outweigh the costs. But I had a suspicion that John didn't have a good handle on his finances overall and once he realised this would be very interested in using the template to rectify the situation.

Luckily the focus of the class that evening was on how to view one's financial health at a point in time. So I asked John if he would record his spending on the Fit Money Workout Template for just next week and we could then have a further chat, although I was pretty certain that the penny would drop before then.

We then went back to the group who had been chatting in our absence about their experiences of the past 7 days and the questions I had posed to them last week. Here is some of their feedback.

Mary – a young solicitor with an image to keep and a young family....

" I was asked last week if it would have saved time if my husband had used the main debit card for spending. Previously he had used a separate account and I had to transfer funds to reflect the expenditure properly in the bank account and template. I know the obvious answer is yes it would have avoided the transfer, but we talked about the move to using one bank account when I got home and it brought up a bigger point. We realised the more straightforward our approach to managing money is, the more likely we are to adhere to whatever guidelines we set. For example up to participating on the course we had been using 7 different bank accounts. I know it sounds crazy but we both had our salaries paid into what were our initial student accounts and they had some direct debits coming out on a monthly basis for cars, insurance etc. We both had saving accounts, which had very little in them based on a small monthly transfer from salaries and used them for socialising and clothes. In addition, we had our joint account into which most of our salaries were transferred and the majority of household payments were made from. The others were a Credit Union account and a special offer account from one of the banks which promised low charges if we kept £1,000 in it but we never got around to using it other than lodging the initial funds. Is it any wonder that we had found it difficult to know where our finances stood? We will certainly be sticking with the one account going forward."

John – single self-employed electrician with a new BMW

"Last week I outlined that I was concerned about spending more money by using a card rather than cash given this was my experience on a night out. I was asked if the debit card approach helped track other spending or could I suggest a different approach. So when I went home I thought about how I might record cash spending on the template. It occurred to me that I could withdraw funds as I needed them and simply keep the receipts to record on the template what I spent my money on. Although the theory was good, in practice I didn't keep all the receipts and when I sat down to input what I had, it just seemed like too much work and so I arrived tonight without a completed template. To be honest I wasn't going to come tonight as I felt I was letting everyone down by not completing the exercise. But then I realised if I didn't stick with the group I would probably never really get a handle on money and I am going to prepare everything that is required for next week."

Jenny – the accountant living at home with parents and working with a global company

"Last week I talked about the real "Need" to be with my friends whilst questioning the choice of very expensive restaurants. I was asked to reflect on whether the Michelin restaurant represented a real "Need" and if I was passing up on anything by using my money for fine dining. When I thought about this initially I felt that given I work hard and have the funds available there was no harm in treating myself. But when I focused on what I might do with an extra £10,000 per year its suddenly dawned on me that after a few years I would have a deposit for my own house. In fact for the first time ever I realised that I have been satisfying a lot of "Wants" ranging from expensive holidays to designer clothes without considering how to work towards the "Need" of having my own house."

Liam – a middle aged Civil Servant with teenage children and older parents

"Last week I talked about the row I had with my wife when we started to look at our spending as it became apparent that the BMW I had "Wanted" was a strain on our budget as was having two holidays per year which my wife had "Wanted". We agreed to move forward by tracking spending for a few months but I was asked to reflect on what effect this might have on our finances and if this might lead to a situation of trying to close the stable door after the horse had bolted. I initially resented that our proposed solution (which had resolved the argument at home) didn't seem appropriate. But when we looked at it we could see that the large repayments on the BMW and the skiing holiday were exactly like bolting the stable door in trying to deal with a problem which had already occurred."

We agreed we needed to get ahead of any potential problems and that we would create a revised plan for going forward which would take "Wants" and "Needs" into account.

I thanked everyone for taking the time to think about the question they had been posed. For me the most interesting aspect of the last week was that their self-reflection had revealed key insights which would undoubtably lead to success going forward. I then gave a real-life example of where lack of planning nearly led to financial disaster before looking at our updated example Fit Money Workout Template which now included a second week of expenditure.

"Thanks John don't be too hard on yourself for not wanting to put the numbers together. Many years ago I was mentoring with the enterprise board and met an individual that nearly suffered financial ruin through lack of basic planning. Dave came to my office supposedly to get an understanding as to how one might put a business plan together. But once the introductions were over I could hardly get a word in edgeways. He had an idea that he would sell writing pens in school colours to children all over the country. They would be sold for one pound each with replaceable ink cartridges and such quality as to be indestructible. He excitedly outlined that sales would be in the millions and had already set up a meeting with a patent lawyer to try and insure no one else could copy the idea. Dave outlined that he had a good job with the same company for the last 20 years but just handed in his notice to leave.

That's where I nearly fell off the chair and stopped Dave to ask a question. I was familiar with people being very excited about their ideas but never before had I met someone who had handed in their notice based on one. Without wanting to alarm Dave I proceeded to ask if any market research had been carried out? He enthusiastically described how his children had taken a one line survey to school asking their friends if they would buy pens in their school colours and got a great response. I asked if the cost of manufacture had been calculated and Dave outlined that the pens would be imported from China and "surely" wouldn't cost very much.

I now had a worrying image in my head of a few months down the road with a bank not being very interested in the reasoning as to why Dave couldn't pay his mortgage. I asked if a sales and distribution model had been worked out and Dave said he was going to buy a van and go from school to school selling the pens. By this time it was clear that Dave had got very excited about his idea and jumped in head first by handing in his notice without a great deal of planning. He was also very nice person with big responsibilities in having three children to rear and a mortgage to pay.

So I "suggested", more like implored that Dave reconsider keeping his job until some more research had been carried out and a business plan put together covering the key operational and financial elements of the proposed business.

The long story short is that about a month later Dave asked to meet me. I thought it was to get some guidance on how to build finances into his business plan but he hardly got in the door before he was thanking me profusely for saving his life. Obviously I hadn't, but when Dave actually looked at the opportunity more he discovered that he would probably sell a lot of top quality pens for 1 pound but that it would cost about 1.50 to import these giving a loss of 50 pence per pen. That was without even considering distribution costs and the fact that Dave also needed a salary to pay a mortgage and feed his family.

The happy ending is that when Dave went back to his

employer, they were delighted that he wanted to stay and I now get one extra Christmas card every year. I guess it just goes to show that the old motto "look before you leap" still holds true. And that my friends, is what the course is all about.

We could create our own motto, "Plan before you spend so you don't have to mend"

Fit Money Workout Template

	Category	Annual Plan	Weekly Plan	Week 1 Actual	Week 2 Actual	To date Actual	To date Plan	Difference
Salary allocated to Household		57,200	1,100	1,100	1,100	2,200	2,200	0
Use of Funds								
School Transport	Regular	884	17	15	15	30	34	4
Movies	Regular	0	0	50	0	50	0	-50
Electric	Regular	1,612	31	0	0	0	62	62
Gas	Regular	0	0	0	0	0	0	0
Child Minder	Regular	0	0	0	0	0	0	0
Maintenance	Regular	0	0	0	0	0	0	0
Mortgage or Rent	Regular	9,308	179	179	179	358	358	0
Online/Internet Service	Regular	0	0	0	0	0	0	0
Phone (Cellular)	Regular	520	10	0	0	0	20	20
Phone (Home) Broadband	Regular	520	10	0	0	0	20	20
Supplies	Regular	0	0	0	0	0	0	0
Personal	Regular	0	0	0	0	0	0	0
Car Loan	Regular	3,484	67	67	67	134	134	0
Hair/Nails	Regular	2,080	40	42	0	42	80	38
Takeaway Food	Regular	520	10	20	20	40	20	-20
Bus/Taxi fare	Regular	0	0	0	0	0	0	0
Fuel	Regular	1,560	30	79	0	79	60	-19
Parking fees	Regular	0	0	0	0	0	0	0
Music (CDs, downloads, etc.)	Regular	0	0	0	0	0	0	0
Sporting Events	Regular	0	0	0	0	0	0	0
Dining Out	Regular	1,300	25	21	21	42	50	8
Groceries	Regular	10,400	200	196	150	346	400	54

Category	Type							
Christmas Gifts & Entertainment	Irregular	1,560	30	30	30	60	60	0
Holidays	Irregular	2,708	52	100	100	0	104	104
Natural gas/oil	Irregular	2,708	52	100	100	200	104	-96
Waste Removal	Irregular	938	7			0	13	13
Water and Sewer-	Irregular	325	6			0	13	13
Health Insurance Family	Irregular	1,781	34	0	0	0	69	69
Home Insurance	Irregular	758	15	0	0	0	29	29
Clothing Kids	Irregular	975	19	40	40	80	38	-43
School Books	Irregular	325	6			0	13	13
School Clothes	Irregular	936	18			0	36	36
Christmas	Irregular	624	12			0	24	24
Sports Club	Irregular	0	0	0	0	0	0	0
Clothing Adults	Irregular	3,120	60	20	20	40	120	80
Extracurricular activities Kids	Irregular	0	0			0	0	0
Medical Family	Irregular	650	13			0	25	25
Dentist	Irregular	130	3			0	5	5
Medical Pets	Irregular	325	6			0	13	13
Holidays Pets - Kennel	Irregular	260	5			0	10	10
Repairs house	Irregular	0	0	0	0	0	0	0
Furniture	Irregular	0	0			0	0	0
Rates	Irregular	867	17	50	50	100	33	-67
Insurance	Irregular	520	10			0	20	20
Repairs	Irregular	390	8			0	15	15
Maintenance	Irregular	520	10			0	20	20

Summary Totals - Spending

Debit Card Payments for Regular Expenses	32,188	619	669	452	1,121	1,238	117
Debit Card Payments for Irregular Expenses	19,812	381	240	240	480	762	282

Summary Totals - Funds left in Bank Account

Funds for Future Investment- Transfer to Depos	5,200	100	50	267	317	200	117
Funds for Future Irregular expenses	0	0	141	141	282	0	282

So lets have a look at what the Fit Money Workout Template should be showing now with 2 weeks of expenditure being compared to plan. You will note that for week 2 I have input regular expenses of £452 versus a plan of £619 which is a saving of £167 for the week.

Given that the plan had £100 built in as a transfer to the Funds for Future Investment we now have £267 to transfer. Taking this with the £50 that was transferred in week 1 we will have moved £317 which is £117 above our initial plan of 100 per week. I have left irregular expenses at the same figure as week 1 at £240 which is £141 below the plan which again appears to be due to timing. The last 2 columns on the right show the to-date figures. We look at these firstly as we want to ensure that spending is in line or below plan when it does come in and secondly that overspending on expenditure is not being masked by under spending in categories due to timing differences. This is particularly relevant for irregular expenditure.

A picture paints a thousand numbers:

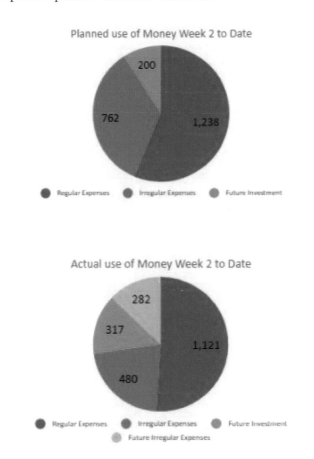

I now wanted to change focus and move to the next stage of the program which is the Fit Money Health Check or a personal assessment of assets and liabilities. Given that we had been having a serious discussion I lightened the approach by going back to our comparison with the person preparing for the 5 mile run.

"My doesn't it seem a long time since you attended the opening seminar? Do you remember our chat about how to take control of your money by viewing it as a tool and that we get the maximum value out of it by training it? We discussed how the first few weeks are hard, its not easy go out and exercise but it helps when you are in a group. At first there is a lot of huffing and puffing but then you start to feel better. Do you see yourself on this journey with your money management? Certainly your feedback tonight leads me to believe you are on the right track.

Hopefully you will also remember from the analogy that it's a good idea to get a health check before taking on anything significant and that we advise a similar assessment of your financial health at this stage. Just like you might not always share what the doctor reveals to you after a health check we do not ask you to reveal the findings of your Fit Money Health Check. In fact we just provide you with the guidance as to how you can carry out this assessment and actions which may be necessary for particular scenarios.

But in keeping with the philosophy of never disclosing anyone's total financial position we do not ask for the results to be submitted. That said we are happy to discuss any element should a participant wish to do so. The following template is our Health Check model.

Fit Money Healthcheck Template	
Assets	**Current Value**
Funds for Future Investment- A/C Balance	0
Savings Account	5,000
Car- Market Value	20,000
Shares	1,000
Boat	5,000
Holiday Home	100,000
Pension Fund	10,000
Total excluding home	141,000
Liabilities	**Amount Due**
Bank Loan	20,000
Credit Card	5,000
Investment Property Mortgage	100,000
Credit Union Loan	10,000
Car Loan	30,000
Total excluding home	165,000
Net Assets excluding Family Home	-24,000

To complete the exercise you need to input into the top section called Assets the key items you own and their value notwithstanding that there may be loans due on some of these. In the bottom section called Liabilities you need to input the various loans you need to repay. The idea is that you are trying to assess if your financial position would allow you to generate through sale of assets, enough money to cover something like a period out of work due to illness or perhaps less worrying but still significant a child's education. There is scope for inclusion of your home in the exercise although many people exclude it on the basis they would never sell it."

"If we look at the Health Check Model presented we can see that excluding the family home the individual concerned owes £24,000 more than they have in assets. A quick scan shows us that they probably have a nice car given the size of the car loan and a holiday home. If this was your friend and you didn't know anything about the debt I bet you would think they were doing very well.

Unfortunately as mentioned earlier not many people talk about debt as they are caught up in the belief that money and the material items which it buys are the defining characteristic of success in people's eyes. They continue to get worse off financially while outwardly seeming to prosper, until it all comes crashing down with an impoverished retirement if not sooner.

You don't have to take my word for it remember the UK Financial Authority survey which outlined over 15 million people have no private pension? But hopefully you can spread the word on the Harvard Research project which dispels this myth and highlights that good relationships are the key to health and happiness.

If we delve a little deeper into our example we can see that the car loan balance is still £30,000 but as happens in the real world the car is worth significantly less than was paid for it. We can see that the holiday investment property has a valuation equal to the loan. We would probably need to know how long they own the property to get the full picture. But assuming its been rented for a reasonable period of time its worrying that none of capital has been repaid.

In the context of good financial management it would seem less than ideal that an individual's pension fund to be worth less than their car. From a liability perspective we can see that there is credit card debt which will have significant interest charges and other bank debt which would have lower charges but nevertheless still compound the problem.

So looking at the total picture we can see that this person is in a poor financial situation and exposed if they had a sudden emergency not to mention lack of funds for the medium and longer term. So what should they do?

Well they need some drastic action to improve their situation but lets save that for next week. In the meantime as well as tracking your spending over the next week you could prepare your own Money Health Check Model. I wont be asking you to share your findings but will answer any questions you may have or indeed review your template if you so wish. No shortcuts now, get the paperwork for both assets and liabilities so you can use the exact figures.

Now tell me about your initiatives and if you have been doing the step challenge.

Mary - the young solicitor with an image to keep and a young family....

"The cost of health insurance has increased dramatically for our family over the past few years. Again its something I never get around to until its too late but last week I took a couple of hours to look at what we are paying and the current offers out there. It seems that I can switch companies and have the same cover with a saving of 20%. A lot of people suggest using a broker so that there is nothing in the small print that leaves you exposed so I am going to go down that route. I still have a couple of months until renewal so there will be plenty of time to double check we are adequately covered."

John – the single self-employed electrician with a new BMW

"My girlfriend and I are going to France on holidays next summer. I needed to book a hire car for the week and my sister mentioned that I could take out excess insurance independently of the rental company. I couldn't believe it as it just took a few minutes online and we saved a fortune and actually have it for the year."

Jenny – the accountant living at home with parents and working with a global company

"I recently paid my annual subscription to my accountancy body and claimed the associated tax relief. I can't understand why so many accountants don't claim this, anyway that's an aside. But it got me thinking that there must be a lot of people not claiming the tax relief that they are due. I looked up HMRC and there is a very straight forward section on "Flat Rate Expenses" which every employee in the country should look at to see if they are entitled to relief to which they are currently not receiving."

Liam the middle-aged Civil Servant with teenage children and older parents

"Last week I mentioned that we have decided to make our home more energy efficient and during the week I started to get some quotes for the work to be carried out. I felt really silly when one of the potential suppliers asked me when was the last time I switched energy provider. I had to admit that we never have as there always seems to be more important things to be done. I then did a little investigation and will save nearly £400 per year by switching."

"Thanks a mil for all the input, I think your initiatives

could really make a big difference to a lot of people. Tell me did you manage to get any steps in?"

The whole emphasis of the step challenge is fun and it seems everyone is always ready for a laugh when we get to the end of the evening. Liam jogged every day for the last week and he was warned that he would need to put more runners into his money spending plan if he kept this rate up! John had bought new runners from the online website Liam used last week. He told us he wanted to get value out of them and so only walked 3 evenings but surprisingly had accumulated 40,000 steps. One of Mary's children was sick during the week and her only regret was that she didn't track her steps on the days she had to take off work as a world record might have been in scope. Jenny mentioned that she felt a bit down having thought about not having a deposit for a house and living at home but that the walking had helped lift her spirits and was back to herself after a couple of days.

CLASS FIVE

DEBT REDUCTION

So by the fifth class of the Fit Money Plan usually most of the participants have developed good money habits. Even those like John who struggled initially now subconsciously bring the "Wants" and "Needs" consideration into buying decisions and save money.

Its important that progress is being made before we start analysing the Money Health Check Template containing a statement of net assets. Invariably given the statistics some people will be in a similar situation to that described previously where on the surface everything looks fine but underneath they are frantically trying to keep going with a big debt burden. The image of a duck comes to mind where everything above the water looks fine but underneath furious paddling is needed to keep going. It may seem counter intuitive to prepare a statement of net assets part way through the course rather than at the beginning, but the logic is if you are already on the road to solving a problem before you discover the extent of it, then the path to success seems much easier.

We don't ask people to submit their Fit Money Health Check Template or present the findings to the group but instead use our previous example and outline how a solution can be found.

"Well how did you get on over the last 7 days, remember there is no need to disclose your financial position?"

Mary - the young solicitor with an image to keep and a young family....

"I know we don't have to talk about our total financial position, but I have to say that the Fit Money Health Check was really a money wakeup call for us. I guess I had this stressed feeling for a while that we might be in the red, but I stuck my head in the sand and got on with the weekly challenge of keeping the show on the road. Unfortunately, the analysis showed we are actually in the red but I feel that our new approach to money management is really going to help. If we can keep in line with our plan to spend less than we earn the 3 credit cards should be cleared in no time."

John – single self-employed electrician with a new BMW

"I would like to talk about my total financial position if its ok with everyone as I was blown away by the exercise for this week. I am a bit embarrassed by the fact that I previously didn't see the point in doing all the work for the Fit Money Workout Template and now find I have a big problem. The truth is I live beyond my means and I never realised it until I put the figures into the Fit Money Health Check Template and chatted to my girlfriend.

To start with I am exactly like the person in the exercise where the car is worth less than the loan I have on it but there is a mountain of other debt as well. I bought a lot of the furniture for the house on Hire Purchase but I didn't think I had a problem as I have been making all the repayments. Unfortunately, when I sat down to look at the numbers I couldn't believe I owed so much on credit cards. I guess I had my head in the sand a bit also. I haven't been able to clear the monthly balance on the credit cards for a good while and just transfer what l have to spare when the bill comes in. I actually took out a few months credit card statements and that made me feel worse as I can see that I also spend a fortune on clothes. Not any more though... you have a new John attending the class."

Jenny - accountant living at home with parents and working with a global company

"Well you will be all glad to know that the accountant's books balanced. Unfortunately that didn't make me feel very good though. I mentioned last week that I had started to think about my buying a house and what the Money Health Check Template revealed to me is that for someone with no commitments I have very little savings. I used to take pride in living within my means but now I don't think I am. The books might balance but someone at my stage with a good income and very few commitments should be putting aside funds for a house deposit and taking some of the balance as disposable income. So don't feel so bad John, there is more than you that had their head in the sand."

Liam – middle aged Civil Servant with teenage children and older parents

"The exercise was good for us, at least we didn't disagree. Obviously myself and John have the same taste in cars and suffer the same reality in the loan being higher than the car value. However on a positive note we were surprised that the transfers into the children's college fund had grown so much. We also bought an apartment 20 years ago and while its been a pain to manage over the years the fact that the mortgage has just cleared helped our overall outlook greatly. It may have distracted our focus though as we also have credit cards which are not being cleared on a monthly basis. I would hate to get into a situation where the apartment had to be sold to deal with these."

I thanked everyone for their input, I was especially interested in the fact that John got a surprise when he took a look at his overall financial situation. But first I reviewed our updated example Workout Template which now included a third week of expenditure.

"So let's have a look at what the Fit Money Workout Template should be showing now with 3 weeks of expenditure being compared to plan.

Fit Money Workout Template

	Category	Annual Plan	Weekly Plan	Week 1 Actual	Week 2 Actual	Week 3 Actual	To date Actual	To date Plan	Difference
Salary allocated to Household		57,200	1,100	1,100	1,100	1,100	3,300	3,300	0
Use of Funds	**Category**								
School Transport	Regular	884	17	15	15	15	45	51	6
Movies	Regular	0	0	50	0	50	100	0	-100
Electric	Regular	1,612	31	0	0	0	0	93	93
Gas	Regular	0	0	0	0	0	0	0	0
Child Minder	Regular	0	0	0	0	0	0	0	0
Maintenance	Regular	0	0	0	0	0	0	0	0
Mortgage or Rent	Regular	9,308	179	179	179	179	537	537	0
Online/Internet Service	Regular	0	0	0	0	0	0	0	0
Phone (Cellular)	Regular	520	10	0	0	0	0	30	30
Phone (Home) Broadband	Regular	520	10	0	0	0	0	30	30
Supplies	Regular	0	0	0	0	0	0	0	0
Personal	Regular	0	0	0	0	0	0	0	0
Car Loan	Regular	3,484	67	67	67	67	201	201	0
Hair/Nails	Regular	2,080	40	42	0	42	84	120	36
Takeaway Food	Regular	520	10	20	20	0	40	30	-10
Bus/Taxi fare	Regular	0	0	0	0	0	0	0	0
Fuel	Regular	1,560	30	79	0	40	119	90	-29
Parking fees	Regular	0	0	0	0	0	0	0	0
Music (CDs, downloads, etc.)	Regular	0	0	0	0	0	0	0	0
Sporting Events	Regular	0	0	0	0	0	0	0	0
Dining Out	Regular	1,300	25	21	21	0	42	75	33
Groceries	Regular	10,400	200	196	150	160	506	600	94

Category	Type								
Christmas Gifts & Entertainment	Irregular	1,560	30	30	30	30	90	90	0
Holidays	Irregular	2,708	52				0	156	156
Natural gas/oil	Irregular	2,708	52	100	100	0	200	156	-44
Waste Removal	Irregular	338	7				0	20	20
Water and Sewer	Irregular	325	6				0	19	19
Health Insurance Family	Irregular	1,781	34				0	103	103
Home Insurance	Irregular	758	15				0	44	44
Clothing Kids	Irregular	975	19	40	40	40	120	56	-64
School Books	Irregular	325	6				0	19	19
School Clothes	Irregular	936	18				0	54	54
Christmas	Irregular	624	12				0	36	36
Sports Club	Irregular	0	0				0	0	0
Clothing Adults	Irregular	3,120	60	20	20	20	60	180	120
Extracurricular activities Kids	Irregular	0	0				0	0	0
Medical Family	Irregular	650	13				0	38	38
Dentist	Irregular	130	3				0	8	8
Medical Pets	Irregular	325	6				0	19	19
Holidays Pets - Kennel	Irregular	260	5				0	15	15
Repairs House	Irregular	0	0				0	0	0
Furniture	Irregular	0	0				0	0	0
Rates	Irregular	867	17	50	50	0	100	50	-50
Insurance	Irregular	520	10				0	30	30
Repairs	Irregular	390	8				0	23	23
Maintenance	Irregular	520	10				0	30	30

Summary Totals - Spending

Debit Card Payments for Regular Expenses		32,188	619	669	452	553	1,674	1,857	183
Debit Card Payments for Irregular Expenses		19,812	381	240	240	90	570	1,143	573

Summary Totals - Funds left in Bank Account

Funds for Future Investment- Transfer to Depos		5,200	100	50	267	166	483	300	183
Funds for Future Irregular expenses			0	141	141	291	573	0	573

77

You will note that for week 3 I have input regular expenses of £553 versus a plan of £619 which is a saving of £66 for the week. Given that the plan had £100 built in as a transfer to the Funds for Future Investment we now have £166 to transfer. Taking this with the £317 that was transferred in week 1 and 2 we will have moved £483 which is £183 above our initial plan of £100 per week.

I have shown the irregular expenses at £90 which is £291 below the plan which again appears to be due to timing. We are not transferring these funds out of the account as the gas and rates bills were paid in the first 2 weeks of the month and we can probably expect the same next month.

As mentioned previously the last 2 columns on the right show the to–date figures. We look at these firstly as we want to ensure that spending is in line or below plan when it does come in and secondly that overspending on some items is not being masked by under spending in other categories due to timing differences. Using our example if we didn't take timing into consideration, we might be tempted to take a view that we are making great progress on irregular spending after 3 weeks in that we have spent £573 less than plan. But when we look at the detail of the line items we can see there is large underspend in the holiday and insurance categories. We know that funds will be required to cover this expenditure at a later stage.

Again we can use our picture paints a thousand numbers concept for an overview.

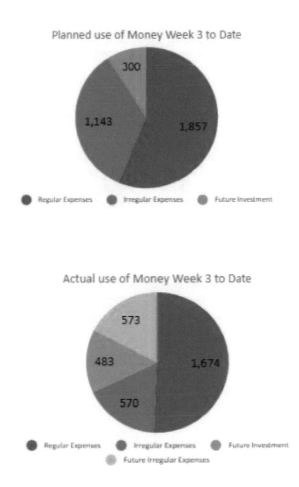

Planned use of Money Week 3 to Date

Actual use of Money Week 3 to Date

Now back to your feedback. It's interesting that John had a big surprise when he put the details together and found out he owed significantly more than he had in assets and the truth is that many people are in that position.

A 2019 TUC report outlined that UK household debt excluding mortgages is at an all time high at £15,385 per household. A Shelter/Yougov 2019 survey indicated that more than half of working renters would not be able to pay their rent for more than one month from their savings. It's probably safe to assume that many with mortgages are in the same situation.

But why is it such a worry if repayments are being made? I guess the first reason is that millions of people are just one piece of bad luck away from serious financial exposure. But at a deeper level research has shown that once in this spiral, the extent of indebtedness is much more likely to increase as we will need to borrow more to service existing debt. It can all happen very quickly. We start off with a college loan which we can't repay until we start working. We get credit cards either in college or during our first job to help pay rent and buy a car. We buy a house and a big chunk of salary is needed for a mortgage so we take more unsecured loans to stay afloat and soon we are like the duck mentioned earlier paddling like mad. So what can we do? Well we can't predict the future but the best way to meet it is on a sound financial footing and the best way to achieve that is to avoid debt.

Don't just believe me, listen to Warren Buffet. You have probably heard of him as the billionaire investor said to be worth $82 billion as per Forbes. He gives interesting talks from time to time and I came across one of his presentations at a conference on the Financial Future of America's Youth which really struck a chord with me. Obviously, he was interested in giving good guidance to young people but he said if he had to give one piece of specific financial advice it would be to stay away from credit cards. "You simply can't make progress in your financial life borrowing money at 18% or 20%. You don't want to be on the side of the equation that's always behind in life and it's way easier to stay out of debt than get out of debt". He summarised by saying if you can't pay for it don't buy it and its fair to say that he generally adopts the same approach with his companies. Possibly as interesting is that down through the ages there have always been warnings about debt even in pre Christian times. Syrus, a Latin scholar, wrote that debt is the slavery of the free.

So with all of these warnings why has debt grown out of all proportion over the last 20 years? It's back to our simple equation of Sales − Costs = Profit. Debt helps companies increase sales and ultimately profit by allowing people who don't actually have money available, to buy products. Credit cards generate even more income for the corporate world in the form of interest paid by the purchaser.

Lets look at a simple example. If a company sells a TV for £500 on a finance agreement they get the base price and possibly 20% extra in interest giving them a total income from the sale of £600. Of course, the downside of this is that the TV with a pay on the day sales price of £500 has actually cost the purchaser £600.

So why do we do this? Unfortunately, it relates back to the same reasoning as we have now discussed on several occasions. Firstly, advertising convinces us that our "Wants" are our "Needs" and secondly that material items have become the defining characteristic of success in many people's eyes. It's often a much bigger expense than a TV, remember my story from the seminar about our affluent clients with the big house and cars that didn't have enough money to get to the end of the month.

I despair a little when I think about the effect all of this has on people but somehow at these times the song "Money cant buy you Love" always comes into my mind. Now, I don't know all the words but it makes me think of all the really important things that money can't buy such as Respect, Manners, Common Sense, Clear Conscience, Purpose in life, Patience, Wisdom, Character etc.

I then think about Professors Waldinger's Harvard project proving that over time the only thing that really matters is good relationships and I become invigorated. I want to spread the Fit Money story to stop the crisis. Hopefully you will also by the time we finish the program.

So now that we all understand that debit is a concern what are we going to do about it? Well the straight answer is to avoid it if possible with the exception of a home mortgage which should be carefully balanced against income and future expectations. We will come back to this in a separate session as for many people a mortgage is often life's biggest financial investment. If we are already on the slippery debt slope or if a little bad luck could put us on a spiral of decline, we need to develop a mechanism for climbing back out of the dependency on other people's money. The key is to change direction and get on the right track so we can develop positive momentum and get better and better. The good news is that we are already well on the road in using the weekly workout template to keep spending in control and tonight we are going to talk about how to use the money health check template to destroy our debt.

There are essentially two approaches generally recommended for reducing debt. The first suggest that we go down the mathematical route and pay off the loans which are carrying the highest interest rate first. The second suggests that we pay off the smallest debt first and get some momentum and feel good factor then move to the next smallest debt.

Now there is no doubt that if you have the determination and resilience to pay 10% of your total debt off every month until its cleared then paying off debts with higher interest rates first will save you money in the long-term. I guess the difficulty with assuming this approach will work is that had a person such determination they may well have avoided getting into debt in the first instance.

Don't feel bad though as there is a big body of research which says it's very difficult to make decisions purely from a monetary perspective. It's called Behavioural Finance and just so we can all feel better, from Oxford to Stanford all the academics agree that psychology has a major influence on the behaviour of investors and financial analysts. In fact Richard Thaler received the Nobel Memorial Prize in Economics for his research in this area. Without getting too complex the area focuses on the fact that people are not always rational, have limits to their self control and are influenced by their own biases.

So how do we overcome this? Well there are now departments in major universities studying Behavioural Finance so you can carry out as much research as you like. But one of the key elements discovered is that we tend to seek immediate gratification. I think we recognise this occurs and that such behaviour can lead to poor financial management. So why not use this bias to our benefit? If we know that we need gratification quickly and we want to solve a financial problem let's get some wins first. Start with the smallest debt and clear it off and then move to the next debt gaining momentum and feel good factor all the time. I am sure that I have done a total disservice to people carrying out PHDs on this topic but we call it the Money Momentum Method and it works.

The real key is to get on the right path and build a good habit to take the difficulty out of self-control. Charles Duhigg, the bestselling author of" The Power of Habit" carried out major research on individuals and companies to understand how implementing key habits can mean the difference between failure and success. Duhigg reiterates MIT research that habits have 3 main factors 1. A Cue - which is the trigger to go into the automatic mode 2. Routine- which is the process itself and 3. Reward -being the reason we are motivated to behave in such a manner. In a similar fashion the Money Momentum Method has 1. A Cue - which is the requirement to have a weekly updated Money Health Check 2. A Routine - which is the process of filling out the template with funds allocated against debt and 3. A Reward - being the positive impact of the results showing a reduction in debt and an increase in assets. So using the example we had previously for the Money Health Check we can arrange the debits from largest to smallest.

Fit Money Healthcheck Template

Assets	Current Value
Funds for Future Investment- A/C Balance	0
Savings Account	5,000
Car- Market Value	20,000
Shares	1,000
Boat	5,000
Holiday Home	100,000
Pension Fund	10,000
Total excluding home	141,000

Liabilities	Amount Due
Investment Property Mortgage	100,000
Car Loan	30,000
Bank -Term Loan	20,000
Credit Union Loan	10,000
Credit card	5,000
Total excluding home	165,000

Net Assets excluding Family Home	-24,000

You are probably sitting there thinking that it all sounds great in practice but where does the money come from? Well hopefully you will remember the earlier Fit Money Workout Template example and the category "Funds for Future Investment" where we transferred the saved £50 in week 1, £267 in week 2 and £166 in week 3 to a bank account set up for this purpose.

At the time we said this money was for investment and we are now going to take that step through using the funds set aside to get a 20% or greater return by paying off credit card debit. The chart on the next page reflects how the Money Health Check Template would look after week 3 having transferred the funds saved initially to the future investment bank account and then using these to pay some
of the credit card debt.

Fit Money Healthcheck Template

Assets	Current Value	Week 1 Value	Week 2 Value	Week 3 Value
Funds for Future Investment- A/C Balance	0	50	267	166
Savings Account	5,000	5,000	5,000	5,000
Car- Market Value	20,000	20,000	20,000	20,000
Shares	1,000	1,000	1,000	1,000
Boat	5,000	5,000	5,000	5,000
Holiday Home	100,000	100,000	100,000	100,000
Pension Fund	10,000	10,000	10,000	10,000
Total excluding home	141,000	141,050	141,267	141,166

Liabilities	Amount Due	Week 1 Due	Week 2 Due	Week 3 Due
Investment Property Mortgage	100,000	100,000	100,000	100,000
Car Loan	30,000	30,000	30,000	30,000
Bank -Term Loan	20,000	20,000	20,000	20,000
Credit Union Loan	10,000	10,000	10,000	10,000
Credit card	5,000	5,000	4,950	4,683
Total excluding home	165,000	165,000	164,950	164,683

Net Assets excluding Family Home	-24,000	-23,950	-23,683	-23,517

Working through the chart step by step we can see the line Funds for Future Investment A/C Balance represents the funds in the bank account set up for this purpose. At the end of week 1 we can see £50 as the balance in the account. In week 2 this £50 was transferred from the future investment bank account to the credit card account and we see that the liability reduced to £4,950. In the meantime in week 2 we can also see a transfer of £267 into Funds for Future Investment account. This is then transferred to the credit card account in week 3 while another £166 is transferred into the future investment bank account.

I realise that £483 (£50+267+£166) over 3 weeks or £161 per week seems like a lot in that it equates to £8,372 per year. So let's be more conservative and say that £100 per week would be more realistic. What could we do with an extra £5,200 per year? Well you might be surprised to find out that it could save nearly £60,000 off the interest cost of an average mortgage or generate £124,000 income over 20 years using a 7% annual rate of return as per the Dow Jones index from 2000 to 2020. But we will come back to all of that in the future, for the moment we just need to develop the habit of getting our money fit.

For next week I would like you to update your Money Health Check Template with the funds you have designated as set aside for investment on your Money Workout Template and transfer the funds to the investment bank account set up for this purpose. I won't be asking you to share your charts with the group but as usual we will discuss the exercise.

Now tell me, how did you get on with your initiatives last week and if you are still stepping it out.

Mary – a young solicitor with an image to keep and a young family….

"It's funny I now find myself just being smarter with money without making any effort. We just booked our summer holiday in France and needed to hire a car also. I thought I might get an early deal but unfortunately its still very expensive. I remembered what John had said last week about getting the excess insurance elsewhere and asked customer service how much I was paying for a satnav. I couldn't believe it when they said that it added £100 to the cost of our rental. Needless to say we excluded that option and will be using our smartphones. Thanks for the prompt John. I wonder how many people just book hire cars without ever asking a question about the fee?"

John – single self-employed electrician with a new BMW

"You will all be proud of me this week as my initiative is very grown up. As you know I am self-employed and if I get injured, I would be very exposed financially. I had an idea that you could insure yourself against injury but always guessed it would cost a fortune. So under pressure to come up with something for the group I phoned the insurance company. I was pleasantly surprised to see that £50 a month would give me significant cover and better again its tax deductible. I know its not saving money but it could be in the long run".

Jenny- accountant living at home with parents and working with a global company

"I mentioned in work during the week that I had come across the HMRC site for flat rate expenses and incredibly not many of the finance team had thought to investigate if they were entitled to anything. You can probably guess what happened next. Like children around a bag of sweets the finance team attacked the HMRC website to see what tax reliefs they might be entitled to. One of the most significant discoveries was that we could claim for use of our own car when traveling on business if our employer doesn't compensate for it."

Liam – middle aged Civil Servant with teenage children and older parents

"We must all be in holiday mode currently. My story this week was really taking the step that we have been putting off for a long time. Several friends of ours have been saving a fortune by swapping their houses for 2 weeks each summer with other families all over Europe. There is a company which arranges the introductions and like trip advisor you can see online reviews of properties which people have stayed in previously. I have always been a little too cautious to go through with it but in the spirit of saving money we have now agreed to swap our house with a couple in Italy for two weeks in June. So the cost of our holiday will be limited to flights and food."

I hardly got to ask about the step challenge before John piped up that this simple exercise was probably having more impact on his life than anything else . When I asked him to elaborate John outlined that getting some air every day had really helped his head and he found that he had more energy to get through work and even complete his Fit Money Workout Template. Everyone else seemed to agree and as it was going to be hard to top John coming on board we called it a night and all went for a walk together.

CLASS SIX

FOCUSED TRAINING – MORTGAGE REVIEW

Class Six is a real milestone as the participants now understand the weekly exercises required to get their money fit. In most cases filling out the Fit Money Workout Template and Fit Money Health Check Template will have become much easier. In truth at this stage the basics have been covered but we continue our program to consolidate the learning and support the formation of good habits. In addition we focus on some of the biggest money decisions people take in life as very often these can be made with a lack of basic knowledge and have huge consequences. I started by chatting to the group about their previous week.

"Well how did you get on over the last 7 days, remember there is no need to disclose your financial position?"

Mary – a young solicitor with an image to keep and a young family….

"At first I didn't like the idea of having to complete two templates each week but I soon realised that the Fit Money Health Check changes very little and is essentially based on the progress I have made in managing my money as reflected on the Fit Money Workout template. We decided to put some of the money we were allocating to holidays against one of the credit cards. My sister has a mobile home in the south east which we can use practically anytime we want. We actually love it as we seem to connect more as a family when we are there. I don't know why we haven't used it for summer holidays before, I suppose it was a "Keeping up with the Jones" kind of thing. I liked being able to say at the school gate or in meetings that our holiday in the Bahamas was perfect. Actually I don't think anyone's holidays are ever perfect and I have come back from many of them needing another! By the way, the concept we discussed last week of little rewards is spot on as I did get a sense of satisfaction in seeing the credit card balance reduce on the Fit Money Heath Check template."

John – single self-employed electrician with a new BMW

"You will remember last week was bad for me as I realised I was living way beyond my means when putting my Fit Money Health Check together. It's funny as I probably also suffered by not completing the Fit Money Workout Template from the start and therefore had less progress to show on the Fit Money Health Check Template when I filled it out for this weeks meeting. I was also surprised that I was less stressed this week even though I now have a full list of what I owe. Somehow that exercise of getting a handle on things and having a plan for moving forward is very helpful mentally even if progress is going to be slow. I do have one big bit of news in that I have agreed to rent a room to one of my mates. I had talked about the tax relief for doing this before but hadn't done anything about it as I didn't like to concept of sharing my house. But I now see that I will have trouble keeping the house unless I can get my finances in order. He is to move in over the weekend and I have asked him to pay on a weekly basis so I can start making inroads to my debts as soon as possible."

Jenny – the accountant living at home with parents and working with a global company

"I shared last week my lightbulb moment of realising I wasn't as good with money as I thought given my lack of savings. I did sit down and look at what a reasonable deposit for a home might be as my ultimate goal would be to buy a nice apartment somewhere reasonably central. Whilst I could probably get on the property ladder and commute with a small deposit and a very big mortgage I think it would be better for me to save a good deposit first. This would have the benefit of helping me reduce my day to day spending and adjust my life style to reflect what will be needed when paying my own mortgage. I also mentioned to the girls that I needed a house in the longer-term more than the short-term satisfaction of a high-class restaurant. We have agreed to spend less socialising going forward and I have a couple of new recruits for the next course."

Liam – middle aged Civil Servant with teenage children and older parents

"When we chatted last week I was happy enough with the exception of credit card debt. When I got home I had a deeper look at the situation and realised that we are paying thousands of pounds in interest on this debt each year. On the face of it we are reasonably financially secure but frustratingly didn't seem to have many levers to deal with the credit card issue. Surprisingly we managed to agree how to move forward without a row. I think it was the Fit Money Templates that made a difference as when we sat down to chat about the issue we had all the information in front of us. Amazingly for us there was no emotion in the discussion as we were simply reviewing facts on a template in a detached rational manner. It soon became obvious that the only option open to sort the issue quickly is to divert the monthly payments to the children's college funds to clear the credit card debit. It will only be a short-term step but will in the long run mean we have more money for college funds as we wont be paying credit card interest."

I thanked everyone for their feedback, it was great to see each participant starting to take real ownership over their finances. I was slightly concerned that Liam's solution was based on reducing investment rather than focusing on lifestyle for a short period of time. I asked Liam if he could have a look at his projected spending to see if there was anything that could be reduced or if income could be increased. Ultimately taking control of the situation was more likely to have a positive effect both financially and mentally.

We then went on to look at the example charts to reiterate how each of the templates should be used and provide a point of reference to support the participants.

Fit Money Workout Template

	Annual Plan	Weekly Plan	Week 1 Actual	Week 2 Actual	Week 3 Actual	Week 4 Actual	To date Actual	To date Plan	Difference
Salary allocated to Household	57,200	1,100	1,100	1,100	1,100	1,100	4,400	4,400	0
Use of Funds	Category								
School Transport	Regular	884	17	15	15	15	15	60	68	8
Movies	Regular	0	0	50	0	50	50	150	0	-150
Electric	Regular	1,612	31	0	0	0	0	0	124	124
Gas	Regular	0	0	0	0	0	0	0	0	0
Child Minder	Regular	0	0	0	0	0	0	0	0	0
Maintenance	Regular	0	0	0	0	0	0	0	0	0
Mortgage or Rent	Regular	9,308	179	179	179	179	179	716	716	0
Online/Internet Service	Regular	0	0	0	0	0	0	0	0	0
Phone (Cellular)	Regular	520	10	0	0	0	0	0	40	40
Phone (Home) Broadband	Regular	520	10	0	0	0	0	0	40	40
Supplies	Regular	0	0	0	0	0	0	0	0	0
Personal	Regular	0	0	0	0	0	0	0	0	0
Car Loan	Regular	3,484	67	67	67	67	67	268	268	0
Hair/Nails	Regular	2,080	40	42	0	42	20	104	160	56
Takeaway Food	Regular	520	10	20	20	0	0	40	40	0
Bus/Taxi fare	Regular	0	0	0	0	0	0	0	0	0
Fuel	Regular	1,560	30	79	0	40	50	169	120	-49
Parking fees	Regular	0	0	0	0	0	0	0	0	0
Music (CDs, downloads, etc.)	Regular	0	0	0	0	0	0	0	0	0
Sporting Events	Regular	0	0	0	0	0	0	0	0	0
Dining Out	Regular	1,300	25	21	21	0	21	63	100	37
Groceries	Regular	10,400	200	196	150	160	170	676	800	124

Category	Type	Annual								
Christmas Gifts & Entertainment	Irregular	1,560	30	30	30	30	30	120	120	0
Holidays	Irregular	2,708	52					0	208	208
Natural gas/oil	Irregular	2,708	52	100	100			200	208	8
Waste Removal	Irregular	338	7				25	25	26	1
Water and Sewer-	Irregular	325	6					0	25	25
Health Insurance Family	Irregular	1,781	34				136	136	137	1
Home Insurance	Irregular	758	15	0	0	0	0	0	58	58
Clothing Kids	Irregular	975	19	40	40	40	0	120	75	-45
School Books	Irregular	325	6					0	25	25
School Clothes	Irregular	936	18					0	72	72
Christmas	Irregular	624	12					0	48	48
Sports Club	Irregular	0	0	0	0	0	0	0	0	0
Clothing Adults	Irregular	3,120	60	20	20	20	20	80	240	160
Extracurricular activities Kids	Irregular	0	0					0	0	0
Medical Family	Irregular	650	13				50	50	50	0
Dentist	Irregular	130	3					0	10	10
Medical Pets	Irregular	325	6					0	25	25
Holidays Pets - Kennel	Irregular	260	5					0	20	20
Repairs house	Irregular	0	0	0	0	0	0	0	0	0
Furniture	Irregular	0	0					0	0	0
Rates	Irregular	867	17	50	50	0	0	100	67	-33
Insurance	Irregular	520	10					0	40	40
Repairs	Irregular	390	8					0	30	30
Maintenance	Irregular	520	10					0	40	40

Summary Totals - Spending

		Annual								
Debit Card Payments for Regular Expenses		32,188	619	669	452	553	572	2,246	2,476	230
Debit Card Payments for Irregular Expenses		19,812	381	240	240	90	261	831	1,524	693

Summary Totals - Funds left in Bank Account

		Annual								
Funds for Future Investment- Transfer to Deposit Acc		5,200	100	50	267	166	147	630	400	230
Funds for Future Irregular expenses		0	0	141	141	291	120	693	0	693

"The Fit Money Workout template should now show 4 weeks of expenditure being compared to plan. I have input regular expenses of £572 versus a plan of £619 which is a saving of £47 for the week. Given that the plan had £100 built in as a transfer to the Funds for Future Investment we now have £147 to transfer. Taking this with the £483 that was transferred in week 1,2 and 3 we will have moved £630 which is £230 above our initial plan of £100 per week.

I have shown the irregular expenses at £261 which is £120 below the plan, again we would assume this is timing related and won't transfer the funds. As mentioned last week it appears that the bills for gas/oil and rates are paid the first 2 weeks of the month and while we didn't spend anything on children's clothing we can expect that a catch up will be needed later. We did see the health insurance and waste removal payments coming out this week suggesting that these bills come through in the last week of the month. This is exactly the point we were making previously as to why the underspend on these categories can't be taken as savings when we know that the expenditure is almost certainly going to occur. Therefore we simply take the view that the £693 delta to plan is money left in the account to cover timing differences. We might take a different view if we were close to the end of the year and it became apparent that there was some actual savings on the irregular spending but for the moment we adopt a cautious approach.

We can however transfer the week 4 Funds for Future Investment of £147 to the bank deposit account set up for this purpose. In addition we can use the £166 which had been transferred into the Funds for Future Investment bank deposit account in week 3 to pay some more off the credit card in week 4. Therefore, the remaining balance on the bank deposit account at the end of week 4 is £147 and the credit card liability has been reduced to £4,517.

All of this can be seen on the following Fit Money Health Check Template.

Fit Money Healthcheck Template

Assets	Current Value	Week 1 Value	Week 2 Value	Week 3 Value	Week 4 Value
Funds for Future Investment- A/C Balance	0	50	267	166	147
Savings Account	5,000	5,000	5,000	5,000	5,000
Car- Market Value	20,000	20,000	20,000	20,000	20,000
Shares	1,000	1,000	1,000	1,000	1,000
Boat	5,000	5,000	5,000	5,000	5,000
Holiday Home	100,000	100,000	100,000	100,000	100,000
Pension Fund	10,000	10,000	10,000	10,000	10,000
Total excluding home	141,000	141,050	141,267	141,166	141,147

Liabilities	Amount Due	Week 1 Due	Week 2 Due	Week 3 Due	Week 4 Due
Investment Property Mortgage	100,000	100,000	100,000	100,000	100,000
Car Loan	30,000	30,000	30,000	30,000	30,000
Bank -Term Loan	20,000	20,000	20,000	20,000	20,000
Credit Union Loan	10,000	10,000	10,000	10,000	10,000
Credit card	5,000	5,000	4,950	4,683	4,517
Total excluding home	165,000	165,000	164,950	164,683	164,517
Net Assets excluding Family Home	-24,000	-23,950	-23,683	-23,517	-23,370

Again using our picture paints a thousand numbers concept the view would be as follows

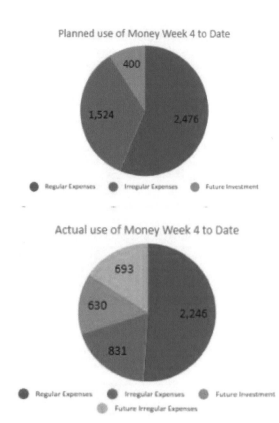

Can you credit it, we are finished? I know you think we have 3 weeks to go but believe it or not you have already been thought our key exercises for getting your money fit. In fact just like the runner in our analogy most of you have, through the weekly exercises already started to get your money into shape.

The truth is we don't have any more templates to

explain or concepts to cover. So why, you might ask, do we continue? Well it's just like the runner in the 5 mile plan. Once basic fitness is achieved, continued focused training is needed to get to the next level otherwise you lose the progress made. Over the next 3 weeks we will monitor the exercises you are putting your money through in the form of the Fit Money Workout & Fit Money Health Check templates to ensure good habits are being developed and the desired success is being achieved. In addition we focus on some of the biggest money decisions people take in life as very often these can be made with a lack of basic knowledge and have huge long-term consequences. Ultimately having managed to get your money fit we want to ensure that you use it properly."

I then had an interactive session where I asked the questions outlined below and the group provided various responses in advance of my summarising the key elements. For ease of understanding I have only included the latter on this occasion.

"For most people taking out a mortgage and buying a house will be the biggest financial decision they will ever make.

How do you think the housing market has changed over the past 20 years? The Office for National Statistics tells us that the median house price in England & Wales was £70k in 1999 and the median earnings were £18k giving a ratio of 3.9 times earnings. In 2009 the median house price in England & Wales was £165k and the median earnings were £26k giving a ratio of 6.3 times earnings. In 2018 the median house price in England & Wales was £232.5k and the median earnings were £29.6 giving a ratio of 7.85 times earnings.

What does this mean? Ultimately that more of our salary goes on housing and in many cases owning a property has become beyond the reach of many people.

How could this happen, surely the Government should stop this? Who gains when the cost of housing becomes so unreasonable? Obviously the bank but let's come back to that. Who else is gaining at our expense? Think about it for a minute.. wouldn't the landowner, the land developer, the builder? And oh.. the government in the form of stamp duty, vat, local authority charges etc. In fact the government has probably gained proportionally more than any other link in the chain from our house price increases over the years.

So what about the banks? Notwithstanding that mortgage rates have been very low for the best part of 15 years the banks also win big on the growing differential between wages and house prices as we need to borrow more to secure a property.

If we take the numbers from our earlier example and assume a 30 year mortgage at a 2.5% interest rate we can see the hidden effect that the increase in house prices has on the total interest payable to the bank. If house prices had remained at £70k and we borrowed 100% today, we would need to repay over the next 30 years £70k capital plus £29.5k interest giving a total of £99.5k. Whereas a £232k 100% mortgage today over the next 30 years using the same criteria would lead to interest repayment of £98k meaning the total repayment required of £330k or £916 per month. Therefore, the picture is much worse than we initially considered as the true house price increase is really £230.5k. (ie £330k todays cost including interest v £99.5k being the 1999 cost including interest) When this is compared to earnings per the Office for National Statistics in 2018 of £29.6k it tells us that the ratio of house price to wages is over 11 times.

Now we all know the rules of the game. It's a capitalist system and the banks wont want to give up their profits or as we said before their shareholders wont want them to. So as usual its up to us to drive the change.

But what can we do? Well the good news is that we can do a lot. In fact this is one of the areas where our new-found money management skills can be put to great effect. Let's say we use our new money management techniques to put aside £100 per week. What effect could this have on purchasing the house in our earlier example with a market value of £232k? Firstly if we saved for 5 years it would give us £26k as a down payment and reduce our mortgage to £206k. If we continued to find this extra £100 per week we could pay £1,350 off our mortgage per month rather than the £916 initially anticipated. This in turn would mean that the £206k could be paid off in nearly 15 years.

Ultimately the total cost of the house would then be £273k made up of £232k Capital plus £41k interest. This is obviously £57k less than the £330k we discussed initially. But we are also mortgage free after 15 years or 20 if you take into account the time required to save the deposit.

That's great I hear you say if I am a first-time buyer but what about the person half way through their mortgage? Well the news is also very good as firstly you could approach your current bank and outline that you have funds set aside and wish to pay more capital off your loan in order to reduce your interest payments. If your bank is not willing to support your new approach to money management, you could always look into switching banks. It would be advisable to use an independent intermediary if switching to ensure you are not exposed by any of the small print.

In addition, when considering buying a house, caution and buyer beware should be at the forefront of your mind from all perspectives. Look at interest rates and consider the effects of fluctuations, sometimes a fixed rate can be worth the peace of mind it provides. Its also worth noting that very few people manage to buy at the bottom of the property market and always be aware of short-term promotions.

Now tell me about your initiatives and if you have been doing the step challenge.

Mary – the young solicitor with an image to keep and a young family....

"They say necessity is the mother of invention and it certainly was for me last week. I had forgotten to book a party in the local play centre for our youngest girl's birthday. I wouldn't mind only it costs a fortune and I was sure we would get a slot. Anyhow I rang one of the other parents from the school to get the details of a children's entertainer they had used earlier in the year for a party. When I called, the lady in question mentioned that the standard rate was £150 for 2 hours but she was unfortunately booked up. Thankfully I had a quick brainwave and asked how she normally ran a party. It seemed to boil down to helping the little girls put on some makeup and teach them some simple dances. When I got off the phone I immediately rang my 16 year-old niece offering her £50 to run the party with the same activities. It couldn't have gone down better, the little girls loved it, my niece loved the money and I loved saving £100."

John – the single self-employed electrician with a new BMW

"I had good luck and bad luck last week. Firstly I broke my phone which was a bit of a disaster initially as clients couldn't reach me. I knew that I was out of contract and would be able to get an upgrade with my current phone provider but one of the apprentices said I should go for a sim only deal and get a separate mobile as it was a much cheaper option. I actually couldn't believe it as the sim only deal with a standard phone is costing me half what my monthly fee would have been if I had gone for an upgrade with my current provider."

Jenny – the accountant living at home with parents and working with a global company

"As mentioned earlier I have decided to get really serious about saving money for a house deposit and so I sold my car. I mostly use public transport and work will pay for taxis if I am required to go to visit clients. I was the typical conservative accountant when setting up the car loan as I structured the repayments to be completed in 3 years. This has turned out to be a real bonus as I used the proceeds of the car sale to clear the rest of the loan and now have £5,000 left to go directly into my savings for a house deposit."

Liam – the middle-aged Civil Servant with teenage children and older parents

"So my initiative generated a lot less money than selling a car but I wish I had discovered it years ago. We normally try to do something as a family once a month and for as far back as I can remember we go for a meal. We decided last week that we would do something else that wouldn't cost as much and we came up with the idea that we would visit the National Gallery in London. I have to say that it was one of the best family days we have ever had. Firstly we only went with the free admission option given the ethos of the day but the rewards were much more than monetary. We actually got to spend some real family time together and whilst everyone's taste differed, we had very interesting conversations. We allowed ourselves chips on the way home so as not to become too highbrow and agreed that we would be more adventurous with our family events going forward."

"Thanks a mil for all the input, your initiatives are all really interesting. It's a big move to sell your car Jenny but it's really given you a huge start on your house deposit. Make sure that you also allocate the insurance costs you would have paid on the car to your house deposit fund. For the rest of the group it's also great to see that the change in mindset invariably leads to lower spending even when looking at needs such as insurance or the phone. I have to say that I am particularly interested in what Liam did last week as not only did the family save money, but they discovered spending time together in an engaging activity can be so rewarding. Tell me did you manage to get any steps in?"

It seemed everyone was enjoying the step challenge and generally completing the 70,000 steps per week. When I asked why everyone was making such an effort it seems that its no effort once you get into the habit. Liam mentioned that the fact that they had agreed to share their achievements each week was the initial incentive to get out and walk but that after only a couple of weeks it was making a difference to his humour and energy levels. Jenny and Mary had actually become good friends through the step challenge as they started to meet at lunch time for a walk. John as per last week had become the step evangelist.

FOCUSED TRAINING – INSURANCE AND PENSIONS

As mentioned in the overview of Class Seven these final weeks of the course are really about consolidating what has been learned to date into good habits and focusing on some key financial decisions. We discussed how to reduce the overall cost of a mortgage last week which obviously could be considered a long-term investment but we are now going to look at the other side of the equation directly and start talking about investing money wisely. After all the course is about getting the maximum value out of our money and not simply a "how to save plan".

This week we talk about term life insurance and pensions, as invariably a large proportion of the population neglect to invest adequately in securing their future. What's even more interesting is that we all know with 100% certainty if we invest in both of these products that we will get a solid financial return whatever happens. If we go early a term life insurance policy will provide funds to meet our commitments and it will be money well spent. Alternatively if we are lucky enough to live a long healthy life we may miss out on a life insurance payment if it's term ends at retirement age. However I don't think many will worry about that when collecting their pension. But before getting into the discussion I asked the group how they fared over the last 7 days and have included their responses below.

Mary – a young solicitor with an image to keep and a young family….

"Last week was hard initially. I think the excitement of learning a new process to help manage money was replaced by a clear understanding of what is required of us to solve our financial situation. We started off the week bemoaning how much it costs us to live and how we would never get ahead but finished the week looking at our budgeted spending from a "wants" and "needs" perspective and felt much more in control. Ultimately we just have to cut back on some unnecessary "wants" to comfortably get our finances in order. In addition to the obvious benefits coming from the analysis of numbers, the templates really help depersonalise money and stop the incessant daydreaming about possible solutions in our heads."

John – single self-employed electrician with a new BMW

"Last week was good for me in that I now have the process of completing both the Fit Money Workout and Fit Money Health Check Template up and running. I was surprised how little time it took, I guess keeping all spending on the debit card is the secret. My new lodger has moved in and he gave me the rent in advance which was great as it allowed me have something to show in funds for investment on the template. It sounds funny to say that I was inspired by an accountant, only joking Jenny. But after listening to Jenny last week I looked into selling the BMW and getting a van for work which I could also use for personal travel. I will have to keep a record of personal use and pay some tax on this but I will still save a fortune. I hope to get the ball rolling on this over the next week."

Jenny – accountant living at home with parents and working with a global company

"I also had a good week. Similar to John I enjoyed the positive effect of being able to allocate more to funds for investment on the Fit Money Workout Template. In my case it was due to no longer having a repayment for a car loan. I went out with the girls on Saturday night to a perfectly nice restaurant and had a lovely time for half the cost of what we have been spending over the past few years. Its funny how the whole "show me" rather than "tell me" concept works. The girls were interested in the idea of the course initially but without even attending one session they are changing their spending mindset. They saw what little difference going to a nice reasonably priced restaurant made to our evening and how much money it saved them. Of course they can't believe that I actually have a roadmap for buying my own property as that is the holy grail to most people my age."

Liam – middle aged Civil Servant with teenage children and older parents

"Last week I mentioned that we were going to divert payments which have been going to the children's education fund to clear credit card debt and I was asked to look at alternatives. I should say that we did feel bad about this option but it seemed the most logical at the time. Ultimately we decided that we would set aside an hour to discuss what we would do if we didn't have this easy option as such. We actually surprised ourselves and came up with a little approach which is worth sharing. When brainstorming ideas we only spoke positively about each option and listed down those which had the most positives. For example I play guitar and gave lessons before we had children. We thought that kicking this off again would be a good idea for the following positive reasons 1. I like playing guitar 2. I like teaching 3. I would like the extra income 4. People could come to the house and I would save on travel cost and time 5. I would have very few expenses 6. I wouldn't need to learn a new skill. This had many more positives than asking for overtime in work which essentially would just provide extra income. Other opportunities discussed such as cutting back on the children's club memberships had no real positives other than the funds saved and so I have decided to start up my little guitar school again."

I thanked everyone for their input and complemented their new approach to getting their money fit. For me the most interesting reflection had been Liam's. His initial proposal of transferring funds which were set aside for future college fees to pay credit card bills would have saved money but may not have been motivational. This has now been replaced by a very positive activity with the immediate reward of income from the students. We then repeated the exercise of previous weeks by looking at the example charts to see what an additional week of input might look like and discuss areas of spending.

"The Fit Money Workout Template should now show 5 weeks of expenditure being compared to plan. I have input regular expenses of £561 versus a plan of £619 which is a saving of £58 for the week. Given that the plan had £100 built in as a transfer to the Funds for Future Investment we now have £158 to transfer.

Taking this with the £630 that was transferred in week 1,2,3 and 4 we will have moved £788 which is £288 above our initial plan of £100 per week. We did have £100 in phone bills in the week which needed to be paid and cut back on some "Wants" to ensure that we could maintain our momentum and transfer a reasonable amount to the Fit Money for Future Investment bank deposit account.

I have shown the irregular expenses at £150 which is £231 below the plan, again we would assume this is timing related and won't transfer the funds out of the account. We see the rates and oil bills coming in as expected in the early part of the new month. Although we have £924 available for future spending on this category we can't become complacent as looking at the individual line items we can see that none of the large expenditures such as insurance have yet become due. We would hope to negotiate monthly payments when agreeing a contract for a new year but we can't assume that will be the case.

We can however transfer the week 5 Funds for Future Investment of £158 to the bank deposit account set up for this purpose. In addition we can use the £147 which had been transferred into the Funds for Future Investment bank deposit account in week 4 to pay some more off the credit card in week 5. Therefore, the remaining balance on the bank deposit account at the end of week 5 is £158 and the credit card liability has been reduced to £4,370. All of this can be seen on the following Fit Money Heath Check Template.

Fit Money Workout Template

	Category	Annual Plan	Weekly Plan	Week 1 Actual	Week 2 Actual	Week 3 Actual	Week 4 Actual	Week 5 Actual	To date Actual	To date Plan	Difference
Salary allocated to Household		57,200	1,100	1,100	1,100	1,100	1,100	1,100	5,500	5,500	0
Use of Funds											
School Transport	Regular	884	17	15	15	15	15	15	75	85	10
Movies	Regular	0	0	50	0	50	50	0	150	0	-150
Electric	Regular	1,612	31	0	0	0	0	0	0	155	155
Gas	Regular	0	0	0	0	0	0	0	0	0	0
Child Minder	Regular	0	0	0	0	0	0	0	0	0	0
Maintenance	Regular	0	0	0	0	0	0	0	0	0	0
Mortgage or Rent	Regular	9,308	179	179	179	179	179	179	895	895	0
Online/Internet Service	Regular	0	0	0	0	0	0	0	0	0	0
Phone (Cellular)	Regular	520	10	0	0	0	0	50	50	50	0
Phone (Home) Broadband	Regular	520	10	0	0	0	0	50	50	50	0
Supplies	Regular	0	0	0	0	0	0	0	0	0	0
Personal	Regular	0	0	0	0	0	0	0	0	0	0
Car Loan	Regular	3,484	67	67	67	67	67	67	335	335	0
Hair/Nails	Regular	2,080	40	42	67	42	20	20	124	200	76
Takeaway Food	Regular	520	10	20	20	0	0	0	40	50	10
Bus/Taxi fare	Regular	0	0	0	0	0	0	0	0	0	0
Fuel	Regular	1,560	30	79	0	40	50	30	199	150	-49
Parking fees	Regular	0	0	0	0	0	0	0	0	0	0
Music (CDs, downloads, etc.)	Regular	0	0	0	0	0	0	0	0	0	0
Sporting Events	Regular	0	0	0	0	0	0	0	0	0	0
Dining Out	Regular	1,300	25	21	21	0	21	0	63	125	62
Groceries	Regular	10,400	200	196	150	160	170	150	826	1,000	174

Category	Type	Annual									
Christmas Gifts & Entertainment	Irregular	1,560	30	30	30	30	30	30	120	150	30
Holidays	Irregular	2,708	52					100	0	260	260
Natural gas/oil	Irregular	2,708	52	100	100	100	0	25	300	260	-40
Waste Removal	Irregular	338	7						0	33	8
Water and Sewer-	Irregular	325	6						0	31	31
Health Insurance Family	Irregular	1,781	34	0	0	0	136	136	136	171	35
Home Insurance	Irregular	758	15	0	0	0	0	0	0	73	73
Clothing Kids	Irregular	975	19	40	40	40	0	0	120	94	-26
School Books	Irregular	325	6						0	31	31
School Clothes	Irregular	936	18						0	90	90
Christmas	Irregular	624	12	0	0	0	0	0	0	60	60
Sports Club	Irregular	0	0	0	0	0	0	0	0	0	0
Clothing Adults	Irregular	3,120	60	20	20	20	20	20	80	300	220
Extracurricular activities Kids	Irregular	0	0						0	0	0
Medical Family	Irregular	650	13	0	0	0	50	50	50	63	13
Dentist	Irregular	130	3						0	13	13
Medical Pets	Irregular	325	6						0	31	31
Holidays Pets - Kennel	Irregular	260	5						0	25	25
Repairs house	Irregular	0	0						0	0	0
Furniture	Irregular	0	0						0	0	0
Rates	Irregular	867	17	50	50	50	0	0	150	83	-67
Insurance	Irregular	520	10						0	50	50
Repairs	Irregular	390	8						0	38	38
Maintenance	Irregular	520	10						0	50	50

Summary Totals - Spending

	Annual									
Debit Card Payments for Regular Expenses	32,188	619	669	452	553	572	561	2,807	3,095	288
Debit Card Payments for Irregular Expenses	19,812	381	240	240	90	261	150	981	1,905	924

Summary Totals - Funds left in Bank Account

	Annual									
Funds for Future Investment - Transfer to Deposit Acc	5,200	100	50	267	166	147	158	788	500	288
Funds for Future Irregular expenses	0	0	141	141	291	120	231	924	0	924

Fit Money Healthcheck Template

Assets	Current Value	Week 1 Value	Week 2 Value	Week 3 Value	Week 4 Value	Week 5 Value
Funds for Future Investment- A/C Balance	0	50	267	166	147	158
Savings Account	5,000	5,000	5,000	5,000	5,000	5,000
Car- Market Value	20,000	20,000	20,000	20,000	20,000	20,000
Shares	1,000	1,000	1,000	1,000	1,000	1,000
Boat	5,000	5,000	5,000	5,000	5,000	5,000
Holiday Home	100,000	100,000	100,000	100,000	100,000	100,000
Pension Fund	10,000	10,000	10,000	10,000	10,000	10,000
Total excluding home	141,000	141,050	141,267	141,166	141,147	141,158

Liabilities	Amount Due	Week 1 Due	Week 2 Due	Week 3 Due	Week 4 Due	Week 5 Due
Investment Property Mortgage	100,000	100,000	100,000	100,000	100,000	100,000
Car Loan	30,000	30,000	30,000	30,000	30,000	30,000
Bank - Term Loan	20,000	20,000	20,000	20,000	20,000	20,000
Credit Union Loan	10,000	10,000	10,000	10,000	10,000	10,000
Credit card	5,000	5,000	4,950	4,683	4,517	4,370
Total excluding home	165,000	165,000	164,950	164,683	164,517	164,370

Net Assets excluding Family Home	-24,000	-23,950	-23,683	-23,517	-23,370	-23,212

Our picture paints a thousand numbers becomes even more useful as the weeks go by.

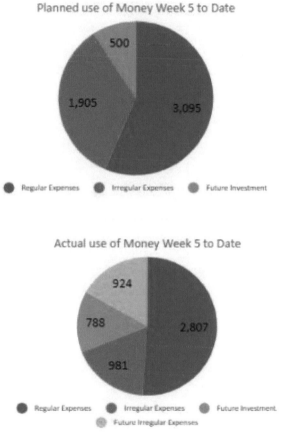

I *then went on to talk about spending money.*

This week we are going to talk about spending our savings. Can you believe it after everything we have gone through to distinguish "wants" from "needs" and track everything from shopping to school books that I am going to ask you to part with your savings? Well it shouldn't be a surprise as the course has always been about exercising your money to get it fit so that it provides maximum benefit to you. In fact, it might not have seemed like it at the time but we have already started to talk about investing wisely. Think back to our discussions on mortgages last week. Didn't we chat about how extra funds generated through our fit money program could be used to dramatically reduce the life of the mortgage and save a huge amount?

This week we are going to talk about investing in life insurance and pensions. Now I know large proportions of the population do not consider these investments but what else are they? If you take out a term life insurance policy and a pension policy you are guaranteed to get money back on one of them. A typical term life insurance agrees to pay a specific amount on the death of the policy holder if it occurs in advance of reaching a certain age, normally retirement.

I know I would be happy to forgo the monetary return on the term life policy in exchange for the peace of mind it gives me now. Term life insurance is probably of most benefit to those with dependants. Close your eyes for a minute, how would your family manage if you left this world early? I know it's not a nice thought and in fact many people avoid considering what might happen because the consequences are so serious. What would it cost to fund a full-time house parent in addition to the current household expenses? Remember that without life insurance this would probably need to be paid out of the after-tax income of one salary. It most cases it would lead to financial ruin. So having considered the consequences term life insurance would appear to be a good investment. The good news is that term life insurance is much cheaper than most people expect. For example one of the most prominent names in the UK is @ 31.12.19 offering life insurance from £10 per month.

What if we did the closed eyes exercise and thought about living a long life but being burdened with an illness which prevented us from working for a number of years. Again I appreciate it's not a nice thing to consider but surely its better than leaving this life early?

Obviously from a personal perspective its easier to contemplate but unfortunately from a financial perspective a debilitating illness may pose an even greater challenge. Not only would the loss of income and the extra cost of a full-time house parent need to be considered but also the additional medical expenses. Fortunately, we can insure against such a scenario and its normally called Income Protection or Permanent Health insurance. For those with no such cover currently, insuring against such events obviously merits serious consideration. But is also a worthy exercise for employees with life cover and permanent health insurance as part of their employment contract. The reason being that the potential pay-outs in the event of illness or death are often less than expected. For example some occupational policies have life insurance cover at one years salary. Would this meet the needs of dependants going forward? Perhaps some additional life insurance cover taken out privately could provide a lot more comfort. The same question could be asked in relation to income protection cover through an employee occupational scheme. What if this only provided salary for 6 months should the employee be unable to work for 5 years? Where would the other 4.5 years income come from? Perhaps it would be worth considering supplementing the occupational scheme with some private health insurance.

Of course, there is the argument that in looking at the statistics it appears insurance is a poor investment as it only provides a return in the unlikely occurrence of a catastrophic event. That said the counter argument is that the devastation likely should such an event occur is so extreme that the peace of mind provided by insurance is a return on investment every day.

We have discussed in detail the importance of Life and Income Protection insurance given large sections of society ignore these options leading to devastating impacts in some cases. But you should also consider what other large financial exposures you might wish to insure against. It's heartening to see that most homeowners take out House Insurance possibly as a mortgage requirement but heart breaking to hear about the cases where they forget to continue with the policy once the mortgage has been repaid and the house is subsequently destroyed by fire. Obviously, that mistake should be avoided as should any inaccuracies when completing the policy documents. Remember if there are issues with the information you provide on the application to the insurance company it could make the contract null and void and result in the non-payment of subsequent claims. Always seek professional advice when taking out an insurance policy or switching between providers as the small print can often be the big issue.

I then switched tack and had a chat with the group about investing in pensions. It's probably the easiest subject to talk about as the numbers are very simple.

An individual just needs to decide what they would like their annual income to be in retirement and there are any number of calculators to determine what level of investment fund would need to be built up under a defined contribution plan to deliver this. The difficulty though is getting people to accept the reality that if they don't make appropriate investments now their lifestyle in retirement will be much reduced.

"Now for Pensions. The good news is that due to

automatic enrolment in the UK a much greater percentage of the population are contributing to pensions than was the case 10 years ago. The bad news is that the projected income from these contributions are well short of anticipated requirements. So how can you ensure you have enough funds in retirement? Actually, its very straight forward. You simply decide what annual income you want in retirement and use a pension calculator to determine what your monthly contribution should be today to facilitate this. The easiest way to set a target is to take a look at your current spending and decide what will not be required when you reach retirement.

Hopefully some of the larger ticket items such as mortgage will be gone away but so should most of the expenditure on children which when taken together can be even more significant. Let's say you decide a good level of income might be the average UK employee earnings in April 2019 of £30,420 as per the Office of National statistics. Using the Money Advice Service Calculator @30.12.19, we can see that a pension pot contribution of £350 per month matched by an employer pension pot contribution of £350 would be required for a 30 year old male to attain this level of income on reaching 68. (including state pension of £8,767 assuming relevant criteria are met). So not only do we have the facts but as of 30.12.19 the Government will also help us by giving tax relief on funds invested in a private pension schemes which broadly add 20%.

You might wonder if its so straightforward, why are so many pensions underfunded? Hard as it may be to believe it comes back to behavioural finance again. Shlomo Benartzi a professor at UCLA Anderson School of Management is a behavioural economist who has studied the underfunding of pensions in detail in the USA where a similar problem exists. He outlines that we are all influenced by present bias in that we know that we should save but the desire for immediate gratification is often stronger and many people spend what they don't have.

So how can we learn to overcome this bias if so many people don't manage to? Actually we already have. Remember the Money Momentum Method where we used our understanding of human nature to create a system which provided immediate rewards by paying off the smallest debt first and supported this with the development of good habits based along the lines Duhigg/MIT had suggested in the form of Cue , Routine and Reward? To achieve success with pension all we need to do is change the emphasis of our proven model. The immediate gratification is received through the commencement of a pension payment and the 3 key elements driving good habits are as follows; 1The Cue; the requirement to have a weekly updated Pension Fund on the Money Health Check. 2.The Routine; the process of filling out the template with the funds allocated to pension and 3. The Reward; the positive impact of the results showing an increase in funds set aside for retirement.

Obviously, the funds must come from the workout model in the first instance but our experience is that whilst it may appear excess funds are not available initially participants generally find the money to make the important payments when the true impact of wise decision making becomes clear.

Now tell me about your initiatives and if you have been doing the step challenge.

Mary – the young solicitor with an image to keep and a young family….

"I can't remember who famously said simple is beautiful but I discovered it last week. We normally try to visit one set of parents each month as it's a four hour drive to mine and similar for my husband. If you have young kids you will know that four hour drives don't exist as between toilet stops, food stops and traffic it often converts to a stress filled five or six. Generally we try to drive for as long as we can get away with before the children are howling for either food or toilet. Invariably we queue for 15 minutes and spend £50 on food and leave 45 minutes later. So with Fit Money in my mind we decided to bring a very basic picnic with soft drinks, sandwiches and crisps which all told cost less than £10. But saving £40 wasn't the best part. The real bonus was that we only had a 10 minute snack & toilet stop and the journey was pleasantly enjoyable."

John – the single self-employed electrician with a new BMW

"I took a look at the HMRC website for allowable expenses which Jenny had mentioned a couple of weeks ago and found a big section on self-employed. Whilst browsing through it I noticed that you can claim relief for a home office but had never discussed this with my accountant. I rang him and he reminded me that I had never mentioned the home office before. It's probably correct as I used to have time to do the paperwork in the unit I rent but now I find that I spend most Saturdays in the spare room doing administration. It seems I can now claim a proportion percentage of the light and heat cost spent on the house against the garage income".

Jenny – the accountant living at home with parents and working with a global company

"I mentioned earlier that I have sold my car. Whilst I will mostly use public transport I am also going to get a bicycle to give me a little more flexibility. I have been aware for some time that my employer operates a bike to work scheme but hadn't looked into it. I had a quick chat with our HR department and it seems that the company technically buys the bike and I pay a rental which is offset against my tax bill. Most employees seem to buy the bike from the company after a few years at open market value which in practical terms is hugely discounted. Its basically a no brainer if you "Need" a bike but possibly a waste of money if you just "Want" one and won't use it."

Liam -the middle-aged Civil Servant with teenage children and older parents

"Not to be morbid but last week we saved £200 by availing of an offer of a free will from our local solicitor. It was something that we had been putting off for a long time and I thought that it would be a nice way of meeting my target of trying to have a new initiative each week. Little did I know that it could be very relevant to most people. The solicitor informed us that if you die intestate, that is without a will, your assets are divided using a pre-existing formula. This can sometimes create complications ranging from bank accounts being frozen for months until the estate is resolved, to people who are not married or in civil partnerships being unable to inherit anything."

"Thanks a mil for all the input. Seemingly it was Benjamin Franklin that said there are only two real certainties in life and they are death and taxes. So I guess its good that you are figuring out how you can plan ahead to deal with both. Enough about that, how did you manage steps wise over the past week?"

As mentioned previously the whole emphasis of the step challenge is fun. We all know that exercise is good for us and the feedback has been that the mental aspect is just as beneficial as the physical aspect. Mary commented that she felt rewarded each time she exercised and that this had replaced the need to reward herself with "Wants" when shopping on a Saturday. Liam added that he saw the exercise as central to the success of the program as it lifted his humour which seemed to create an openness to the new approach. John checked that everyone had made their target for the week and I joined the group for a walk to finish up the evening.

CLASS EIGHT

INVESTMENTS

By Class Eight of the Fit Money Plan participants generally understand their finances and where they want to get to over the short and medium term. Most will already know that the topic for the week is investment and are eager to understand how they can make their millions. Few will have really appreciated that we have been talking about major investment returns throughout the course. It regularly comes as a surprise that the non-exciting world of paying off a credit card, mortgage or availing of tax relief on pension funding offer a much better return on investment than most of the alternatives. So the first thing we do is re-emphasise the opportunities which should be considered in the first instance. Making the assumption that our participants will maximise these opportunities in the medium term we go forward to discuss the various strategies adopted by major investors of our time. But firstly we get feedback on how everyone fared over the past seven days. "So how was your week?"

Mary - a young solicitor with an image to keep and a young family....

"We had a good week. It didn't take a lot of time to fill out the templates and we put aside the amount we had planned for future investment. Given we are coming to the end of the program I thought a lot about the key elements for me. I think ultimately viewing money as an asset to be used in the best way possible made a fundamental difference. I thought we needed to have more money to enjoy ourselves but in fact I now think it would be a hindrance as we would simply be pulled more into the world of "Wants". The program has challenged us to look at different ways of enjoying ourselves and whether it was intended or not we have engaged a lot more together as a family. Picking up on Liam's train of thought we went to the Museum of London Docklands for free last weekend and had wonderful conversations about it for the rest of the week."

John – single self-employed electrician who used to have a BMW

"I sold my car which was a good news story in that I managed to find a person who was really interested in all the extras I had added and also willing to pay more than I anticipated getting. I still owe £3,000 on a car loan but this will be cleared in 6 months as I will continue paying the £500 per month as before. I also bought a new van through the business which has even more advantages than I first envisaged. At a basic level the monthly payments will come out of the garage income rather than my after-tax salary and so will the diesel for business trips. I know I could have claimed these trips when I was using the car for business purposes, but I never got around to it and the van will just be much more straightforward. I too was reflecting on the course and I think the biggest benefit for me was that I got my head out of the sand and realised that when it comes to money management following the crowd is unlikely to have a good outcome. The actual roadmap of how to create a secure financial future really gives me the confidence that it's the right path."

Jenny- accountant living at home with parents and working with a global company

"I had a good week as we booked our summer holiday. Now before you all start giving out to me we are renting an Airbnb in Biarritz in France and have got a great rate by booking well in advance. In addition we booked flights early and won't need to hire a car so the holiday will probably cost half of last years. I think my reflection on the program is that I have discovered that there is a world of difference between understanding money and behaviour with money. Clearly I have been trained to understand money but my behaviour didn't reflect that. The exercises we performed on the program left no hiding place in that there is a pretty clear path to becoming financially secure and I was not on it. That said I do believe the changes I have made in my <u>behaviour</u> will be good life habits going forward and I am confident facing the future."

Liam – middle aged Civil Servant with teenage children and older parents

"Sorry to bring things down but I didn't have a good week. My dad wasn't very well. He has needed a hip replacement for a while but is on a waiting list with the NHS. We looked into trying to fund it privately and it's just not an option for our family given the costs involved. I didn't appreciate the real-life impact of not having health insurance especially in old age when we were discussing it a few weeks ago but I wish my Dad had it now. Regarding my views on the course, I have actually thought a lot about it over the last few weeks. I find it hard to believe that its relatively straightforward to manage money and yet so many people struggle. I guess it comes back to what we discussed very early in play in that there are no profits to be made in telling the public to be careful with their money. I don't know how you get this story to the masses but it certainly needs to be told, especially to kids as they are bombarded with all sorts of marketing on an hourly basis. If you are told ten times a day that a particular phone or item of clothing is going to make you look cool and feel good it's hard not to believe it. Unless you are given the full picture, like the Fit Money program has provided us with. So that's where I am going to start, by giving my kids the full picture."

I thanked everyone for their input and we then took a look at the example charts to see what an additional week of input might look like and discussed areas of spending.

"The Fit Money Workout template should now show 6 weeks of expenditure being compared to plan. In our example I have input regular expenses of £691 versus a planned spending of £619 which is a overrun of £72 for the week. Given that the plan had £100 built in as a weekly transfer to the Funds for Future Investment we now have only £28 to move. Taking this with the £788 that was transferred in week 1,2,3,4 and 5 we will have moved £816 which is £216 above our initial plan of £100 per week.

We did have £150 electricity bill in the week which could have been significantly off set by not dining out and eliminating takeaway food. But we are ahead of plan and can see from the line item details that there are no real issues. That said we can see there was nothing set aside for movies initially and we have already spent £150. We should make sure that some other social activity is reduced to compensate for this "Want" as we wouldn't want to get into a situation where funds which are required for something like fuel have been spent on entertainment. I have shown the irregular expenses at £550 which is £169 over the plan. This had been expected, haven't we discussed each week that whilst we were spending less than plan we still believed the funds would be required for the future? In week 6 we can see that we have spending in three categories which we haven't seen previously namely £100 on school books, £100 on school clothes and £100 on maintenance. Therefore, instead of putting money aside we are actually using up some of our buffer.

You will remember after week 5 we had ringfenced £924 for future spending in the irregular category and so our £169 over run brings us back to having £755 set aside. Looking at the line item detail for possible issues going forward we can see that there has been no fee paid yet for Home Insurance. This may mean that an annual once off payment in advance has been made previously and we need to keep funds aside to cover this at renewal time. Unless we are certain that the payment structure can be changed to a monthly (pay as you go) basis from renewal time. Should we be able to do this the funds set aside could then be deemed savings and transferred to the funds for Future Investment bank deposit account.We can however transfer the week 6 Funds for Future Investment of £28 to the bank deposit account set up for this purpose. In addition we can use the £158 which had been transferred into the Funds for Future Investment bank deposit account in week 5 to pay some more off the credit card in week 6. Therefore, the remaining balance on the bank deposit account at the end of week 6 is £28 and the credit card liability has been reduced to £4,212. All of this can be seen on the following Fit Money Templates.

Fit Money Workout Template

	Annual Plan	Weekly Plan	Week 1 Actual	Week 2 Actual	Week 3 Actual	Week 4 Actual	Week 5 Actual	Week 6 Actual	To date Actual	To date Plan	Difference
Salary allocated to Household	57,200	1,100	1,100	1,100	1,100	1,100	1,100	1,100	6,600	6,600	0
	Category										
Use of Funds											
School Transport	Regular	884	17	15	15	15	15	15	15	90	102	12
Movies	Regular	0	0	50	0	50	50	0	0	150	0	-150
Electric	Regular	1,612	31	0	0	0	0	0	150	150	186	36
Gas	Regular	0	0	0	0	0	0	0	0	0	0	0
Child Minder	Regular	0	0	0	0	0	0	0	0	0	0	0
Maintenance	Regular	0	0	0	0	0	0	0	0	0	0	0
Mortgage or Rent	Regular	9,308	179	179	179	179	179	179	179	1,074	1,074	0
Online/Internet Service	Regular	0	0	0	0	0	0	0	0	0	0	0
Phone (Cellular)	Regular	520	10	0	0	0	0	50	0	50	60	10
Phone (Home) Broadband	Regular	520	10	0	0	0	0	50	0	50	60	10
Supplies	Regular	0	0	0	0	0	0	0	0	0	0	0
Personal	Regular	0	0	0	0	0	0	0	0	0	0	0
Car Loan	Regular	3,484	67	67	67	67	67	67	67	402	402	0
Hair/Nails	Regular	2,080	40	42	0	42	20	20	30	154	240	86
Takeaway Food	Regular	520	10	20	20	0	0	0	0	40	60	20
Bus/Taxi fare	Regular	0	0	0	0	0	0	0	0	0	0	0
Fuel	Regular	1,560	30	79	0	40	50	30	30	229	180	-49
Parking fees	Regular	0	0	0	0	0	0	0	0	0	0	0
Music (CDs, downloads, etc.)	Regular	0	0	0	0	0	0	0	0	0	0	0
Sporting Events	Regular	0	0	0	0	0	0	0	0	0	0	0
Dining Out	Regular	1,300	25	21	21	0	21	0	70	133	150	17
Groceries	Regular	10,400	200	196	150	160	170	150	150	976	1,200	224

Category	Type	Annual	Monthly							Paid	Budget	Diff
Christmas Gifts & Entertainment	Irregular	1,560	30	30	30	30	30	0	30	150	180	30
Holidays	Irregular	2,708	52	0	0	0	0	0	0	0	313	313
Natural gas/oil	Irregular	2,708	52	100	100	100	0	0	100	400	313	-88
Waste Removal	Irregular	338	7	25	0	0	0	0	0	25	39	14
Water and Sewer-	Irregular	325	6	0	0	0	0	0	0	0	38	38
Health Insurance Family	Irregular	1,781	34	136	0	0	0	0	0	136	206	70
Home Insurance	Irregular	758	15	0	0	0	0	0	0	0	88	88
Clothing Kids	Irregular	975	19	40	40	40	0	0	0	120	113	-8
School Books	Irregular	325	6	0	0	0	0	0	100	100	38	-63
School Clothes	Irregular	936	18	0	0	0	0	0	100	100	108	8
Christmas	Irregular	624	12	0	0	0	0	0	0	0	72	72
Sports Club	Irregular	0	0	0	0	0	0	0	0	0	0	0
Clothing Adults	Irregular	3,120	60	20	20	20	20	0	20	100	360	260
Extracurricular activities Kids	Irregular	0	0	0	0	0	0	0	0	0	0	0
Medical Family	Irregular	650	13	50	0	0	0	0	50	100	75	-25
Dentist	Irregular	130	3	0	0	0	0	0	0	0	15	15
Medical Pets	Irregular	325	6	0	0	0	0	0	0	0	38	38
Holidays Pets - Kennel	Irregular	260	5	0	0	0	0	0	0	0	30	30
Repairs house	Irregular	0	0	0	0	0	0	0	0	0	0	0
Furniture	Irregular	0	0	0	0	0	0	0	0	0	0	0
Rates	Irregular	867	17	50	50	50	0	0	50	200	100	-100
Insurance	Irregular	520	10	0	0	0	0	0	0	0	60	60
Repairs	Irregular	390	8	0	0	0	0	0	0	0	45	45
Maintenance	Irregular	520	10	0	0	0	0	0	100	100	60	-40

Summary Totals - Spending

	Annual								Paid	Budget	Diff
Debit Card Payments for Regular Expenses	32,188	619	669	452	553	572	561	691	3,498	3,714	216
Debit Card Payments for Irregular Expenses	19,812	381	240	240	90	261	150	550	1,531	2,286	755

Summary Totals - Funds left in Bank Account

Funds for Future Investment- Transfer to Deposit Acc	5,200	100	50	267	166	147	158	28	816	600	216
Funds for Future Irregular expenses		0	141	141	291	120	231	-169	755	0	755

Fit Money Healthcheck Template

Assets	Current Value	Week 1 Value	Week 2 Value	Week 3 Value	Week 4 Value	Week 5 Value	Week 6 Value
Funds for Future Investment- A/C Balance	0	50	267	166	147	158	28
Savings Account	5,000	5,000	5,000	5,000	5,000	5,000	5,000
Car- Market Value	20,000	20,000	20,000	20,000	20,000	20,000	20,000
Shares	1,000	1,000	1,000	1,000	1,000	1,000	1,000
Boat	5,000	5,000	5,000	5,000	5,000	5,000	5,000
Holiday Home	100,000	100,000	100,000	100,000	100,000	100,000	100,000
Pension Fund	10,000	10,000	10,000	10,000	10,000	10,000	10,000
Total excluding home	141,000	141,050	141,267	141,166	141,147	141,158	141,028

Liabilities	Amount Due	Week 1 Due	Week 2 Due	Week 3 Due	Week 4 Due	Week 5 Due	Week 6 Due
Investment Property Mortgage	100,000	100,000	100,000	100,000	100,000	100,000	100,000
Car Loan	30,000	30,000	30,000	30,000	30,000	30,000	30,000
Bank -Term Loan	20,000	20,000	20,000	20,000	20,000	20,000	20,000
Credit Union Loan	10,000	10,000	10,000	10,000	10,000	10,000	10,000
Credit card	5,000	5,000	4,950	4,683	4,517	4,370	4,212
Total excluding home	165,000	165,000	164,950	164,683	164,517	164,370	164,212
Net Assets excluding Family Home	-24,000	-23,950	-23,683	-23,517	-23,370	-23,212	-23,184

Our final picture is a really good one.

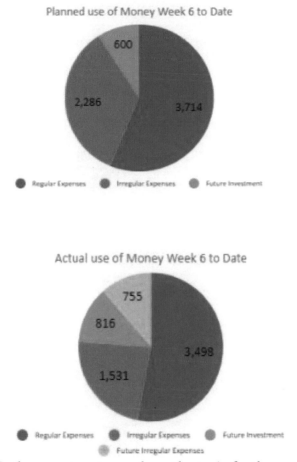

We then went on to speak on the topic for the evening which was investment.

"Its hard to believe it's the final stages of the course already and yet you have achieved so much in such a short period of time. The course is designed to provide a pathway to financial freedom and I am confident given your efforts over the past number of weeks that you are now well on your way.

I know that you have all been eagerly awaiting our investment discussion but if you think about it for a minute we have actually been talking about major financial returns throughout the course. Let's talk about credit cards for a minute. Can we agree that a 20% rate of interest is not unusual on outstanding balances? Is it fair to say that avoiding this interest payment will mean that there is more money in our bank account? Isn't more money in our bank account the idea behind investing?

Remember our discussion about mortgages. Didn't we see in the example that if we could find £100 per week that we could save £57,000 in interest over the life of the mortgage? Now that's a fair return in anyone's language. And what about the tax relief on pensions? I know that many people like to give out about the Government but adding 20% to our investment straight away must be viewed as a significant return. Not only that but these 3 options pretty much guarantee big returns.

Now I don't want to burst anyone's bubble about the complexities of investing. But if we can get a 20% return with these mundane options, we will be doing better than top investor Warren Buffet.

So lets say we have exhausted all these easy options for making big guaranteed returns and want to take our chances with the stock market. Who would we like to emulate?

I guess we should mention Warren Buffet first as he is considered one of the greatest investors of all time. He credits working with Benjamin Graham and his book the "The Intelligent Investor" as having provided the strategy for value investing which he has employed to great effect throughout his career. He told Forbes in September 2017 that "the strategy is to find a good business--and one that I can understand why it's good--with a durable, competitive advantage, run by able and honest people, and available at a price that makes sense. Because we're not going to sell the business, we don't need something with earnings that go up the next month or the next quarter; we need something that will earn more money 10 and 20 and 30 years from now. And then we want a management team we admire and trust." In addition, he has constantly said that the underlying factor in his overall investment success has been compounding. Simply put if you continue to invest your profits over time it will dramatically improve your wealth. For example if rather than purchasing a new car you decided to invest £50,000 now in a fund generating 10.5% it would compound to £1,000,000 over the next 30 years.

On the opposite end of the scale George Soros was seen as a short-term speculator. He made large highly-leveraged bets on the direction of the financial markets. He is most commonly known as the man who "broke the Bank of England". In September 1992, he risked $10 billion on a single trade when he shorted the British Pound believing it was priced too high against the Deutschmark. He was right, and in a single day made over $1 billion.

But the other side of betting big is that you can lose big and it is said that he lost billions in the tech bubble collapse in 1999. That said he has been very successful over 30 years even though some would describe his strategy as gambling rather than investing (Daily Telegraph – 2018). Less widely known is that he has given much of his wealth to charity and now spends a lot of time promoting good causes. He wrote a book in 1986 "The Alchemy of Finance: Reading the Mind of the Market" which outlines his approach of defying conventional wisdom to deliver incredible returns. If you think you can emulate George Soros its going to be of great interest to you.

Somewhere in the middle of the appetite for risk scale lies Jack Bogle. He founded the Vanguard Investment Group in 1974 and built it into a giant mutual fund company, with $4.9 trillion in assets under management. His theory was that its very hard to beat the stock market performance by picking individual stocks so he set up a business that would (in theory) buy shares in every company on the stock exchange. So while the value of the overall investment would fall when one company invested in did poorly it would increase as others did better. Over time this strategy has proved to be very successful as the stock market continued to grow.

The New York Times outlined in his obituary of January 2019 that his philosophy is hard to argue with.

"Since 1984, less than half of the actively managed mutual funds that invest in a broad array of American stocks have outperformed the Vanguard 500 Index Fund".

Surprisingly it seems that Warren Buffet broadly agrees with this philosophy as notwithstanding that he has been great at picking winning stocks he has instructed his charity trustee on his death to put 90% of his wealth into low-cost S&P 500 index fund. Jack Bogle's book, "Common Sense on Mutual Funds" demonstrates how an amateur with a reasonable approach can generate major returns in the long-term.

So there you have it. Once you have gained the large returns on repaying credit card debit, paying off your mortgage early and making tax incentive pension contributions you can start to study the great investors and their strategies to try and beat deposit interest rates. Most of the top investors have written books so there is plenty of research material, I have mentioned three but there are many more.

Now for the last time tell me about your initiatives."
Mary - the young solicitor with an image to keep and a young family....

"I am afraid that my final initiative is very simple in that I am availing of a new electricity discount tariff which comes into effect after 9pm at night. I can run my dishwasher, tumble dryer and washing machine for a couple of hours before bedtime and make significant savings. I make sure they are finished before going to sleep though as there has been a lot of talk about house fires caused by white goods."

John - the single self-employed electrician who used to have a BMW

"I got a fuel card for the new van. I never bothered with this before because I felt it wasn't worth it but in truth it serves 2 purposes. Firstly I can get a report which neatly summarises expenditure rather than keeping hundreds of small slips of paper and secondly I get points for all the fuel I buy. I know that this will only generate small money but I have a new view on savings given our discussion on how £100 extra per week can literally change your life. For me small savings now offer big opportunities."

Jenny -the accountant living at home with parents and working with a global company

"I spent more last week than I planned but I think it's a good thing. Basically, I have been making the minimum contribution of 1% of my gross salary to my pension and my employer has been matching this. A group of us were chatting during week and it seems that most other people contribute 5% of their gross salary as the company will match an individual's contribution up to this level. I put the numbers together and between the additional employer contribution and tax relief at a 5%

level, I could get more into my pension than my own extra contribution. You could say its free money. Obviously I instructed our payroll department to make the changes with immediate effect."

Liam – the middle-aged Civil Servant with teenage children and older parents

"Actually, last week's savings fell into my lap. Our home insurance was up for renewal and I adopted the same strategy as we discussed on health insurance a few weeks ago and phoned around to see if I could get a better offer. I guess I wasn't surprised that it initially seemed I could get several cheaper options, but I asked for the policy details as I was afraid that there might be exclusions in the small print that could come back to haunt me. Given that everything has to be turned around pretty quickly I also phoned back my current provider and told them the other offers I had received from their competitors. To my amazement they said that they would match the lowest offer if I signed up within the next 24 hours. Now I know I may have saved even more by waiting for the other policies to arrive and having a broker look through them, but I took the easy option of 15% reduction without any extra effort. I couldn't believe it as we have been in the house for 10 years and I never thought to phone around before, I simply thought all these companies would need to be competitive on price."

I then closed the course with the following brief synopsis.

"Thanks for your input, it's just amazing how your change in mindset led to new initiatives each week. You will be glad to know that we are just about finished this part of your journey. We created the framework to get your money fit and facilitated a fun activity to get your body fit. It's inspirational that you have made a success of both and are now truly on the road to Financial Freedom.

I think I started the seminar with a question so it's probably appropriate that I finish with a question also.

So what would you do if you achieve Financial Freedom and have more money than you need? Would you follow the consumer culture created by Bernes and be driven by "Wants" rather than "Needs"? Would you seek immediate gratification and act irrationally as all our friends in Behavioural Science might suggest? Or would you be inspired by the words of the Gospels from two thousand years ago "If you wish to be complete, share with the poor"? I don't actually want your answer, its simply for you to contemplate. But don't decide too quickly as you may just get the choice and it seems given the opportunity many people act in a different manner than we might expect.

Take our successful investors mentioned earlier for example. Warren Buffet in 2006 pledged to give all his wealth away over time and since that date has donated more than £34.5 billon. George Soros has given away more than 80% of his net worth to charity and Jack Bogle set up his company is such a way as to be owned by those who invested in the funds rather than becoming a billionaire."

EPILOGUE

We know that all work and no play makes for a dull day. So before letting our participants back into the world of mass marketing, we ask that they set a long-term goal of saving five hundred pounds to undertake a once in a lifetime trip and report back to the group when it is completed. I have included the updates from our group below.

Jenny - the accountant living at home with parents.

I kept up my routine of regular walks after the course finished and even joined a hill walking club with a friend. I think I was lucky because the group I joined were very active and before long I was learning about mountains and had climbed Bennevis. Or rather we walked up the path!

I guess that's why I wasn't phased when one of the most experienced hikers mentioned that he would be taking a group up Mount Blanc for a Summer Challenge. I was told I needed to be fit and a good gauge would be to do a half marathon in two hours. Never one to shirk a challenge I got to work on raising my fitness levels and after a few weeks I was really into my stride. I have to say that I thought all the running was a bit much but I was glad when we got to the mountain.

We went the "Gouter Route" in July which is supposed to be the easiest. Boy, would I hate to see it in September if July is meant to be easy. The first part took us to the Tete Rousse hut. This stage was relatively easy although I was a little nervous when I saw the fixed steel ropes as aids to traverse some dangerous sections. I am not sure if you are supposed to think about falling, but I did and even went as far as considering what might happen if I was killed. For a little while I thought about turning back but as the Gouter hut/hostel was in sight it was obvious that the easier option was to keep going.

Its amazing how a good nights rest can change things as when I awoke the following morning I had a completely different mindset. (note to self - when narky go to bed). After breakfast I simply took one look up the mountain and decided that it was probably going to be as dangerous going down as going up and put my fate in the hands of God, and the various aids and plan b's that could be called on if needed.

It took hours to get to snow where it was easier to walk although as we increased our altitude it became much more difficult to breathe. The thin air made it feel like I was inhaling through a mask and progress became very slow. Stretches which would have taken 10 minutes at sea level were now taking half an hour to complete. Luckily the weather was good and the views spectacular, so when we stopped frequently for a rest, I filled my mind as well as my lungs.

The real challenge of the second day was the "Bosses Ridge" as you are very exposed due to the sheer drops on both sides. Thankfully our weather was good again, but I dread to think what it might be like to get caught out in a breeze up there never mind a storm. Although it was a struggle with many stops we were constantly motivated by our guide's mantra that you can climb any mountain if you keep putting one foot in front of the other. We eventually managed to make it to the top with slow-motion steps.

Reaching the summit was like nothing I had ever experienced before and for a few seconds it was as if the clock stopped. As we stood in silence looking out over snow-capped mountains it was as if all the world was at peace and the complete silence enveloped me to create an inner calm I didn't think possible. In that moment I realised that my life is but a breath of air in the context of this landscape which hasn't changed in millions of years and with that my worries became insignificant.

We descended carefully and got back to the "Gouter Hut" by 7pm. I have never enjoyed a beer so much and to wake up to a fall of snow the following morning covering most of the mountain below us was a beauty to behold. My joy was short lived when our guide told us that the descent through the snow would be the most difficult part of our challenge. In fact, I have since learned that most fatalities occur when descending a mountain even when the terrain hasn't changed as was our dilemma. Thankfully our guide was very experienced and literally showed us every step through the difficult stretches and the beer that night surpassed even the evening of the assent. Having achieved my goal but realising along the way what could go wrong made the relief of being back at sea level all the better.

I still look in awe at the pictures from time to time and nearly have to convince myself that I am the one in the red hat. I know that I will probably never climb a higher mountain but my brief adventure gave me a little insight into what Edmund Hillary meant when he said "Its not the mountain we conquer but ourselves". On a sunny day in a small village in France as I packed my bags to go back to London the penny dropped that I could climb all the mountains of life if I continued to put one foot in front of another.

John - the single self-employed electrician.
I started working fulltime as an apprentice at sixteen and never really stopped to do anything for myself. Ok I

bought a car and took out a mortgage on a house but for the most part that was simply following the next step along the path of life.

I initially thought that I wouldn't bother with the idea of setting aside funds for a once in a lifetime trip as to be honest I don't think that way. But a good friend of mine passed away and I started to realise that life can be short. Then in the uncanny way that these things can happen my cousin asked if I would be interested in driving from Spain to Russia on my old motorbike. I initially thought I couldn't take the time off work and then that it would cost too much but my cousin had carried out a lot of research and the plan was to bring tents and camp each night of the trip.

All was good until a week before we were due to depart when my cousin broke his wrist and was unable to ride his motorcycle. In one of those rare moments for me I decided to be impulsive and go on my own but boy was I apprehensive as I boarded the ferry from Portsmouth to Santander in Spain.

I could probably write a book on my little European expedition, but the highlights would be the people I met and confidence gained along the way. I have described below a few days of the trip to give you a flavour of my experience.

I got into Lemans in France after dark one evening and couldn't find the campsite I had booked or an alternative. I pulled in at a petrol station and asked the other customers for directions in my pidgin French. Whilst many people stopped and tried to help I couldn't understand their responses. Eventually it was clear that one lady knew where the campsite was but not unsurprisingly (in hindsight) vanished when I offered her twenty pounds to let me follow her.

Completely deflated I had decided that I would pitch my tent in a carpark (absolutely not my cup of tea) when a young boy on a scooter asked in perfect English if I needed help. He told me the campsite was on his way home and I could follow him. Unbelievably after all the anguish I was checked in within 5 minutes of leaving the petrol station. The relief was like winning money. Then amazingly the boy (Pierre) arrived back to the campsite with his Dad and invited me to their home for dinner. I couldn't believe their hospitality and we had a glorious meal with wonderful wine and stories to match. They insisted that I spend the night in the comfort of their spare room and I was only sorry to be moving on the next day.

It rained all the way to Belgium and there was only one other camper when I arrived at the campsite in Namur which appeared unchanged since 1950 and as I was to learn was being run by the third generation of the same family. I decided to take a little walk and before long came across the restaurant which looked beautiful but closed.

I was about to turn back to pitch my tent when a middle-aged lady appeared from nowhere and asked me in a friendly Anglo German accent if I wanted a beer. It seemed rude to refuse and what followed was one of the best nights of the trip as Lina (clearly the matriarch) summoned all the family from grandfather to granddaughter to the bar. We sang songs, played games and I vaguely remember some traditional dancing. I don't know whether I was the entertainment or was being entertained but as the Heineken flowed everyone seemed to be having a good time.

It was only at the end of the night when I couldn't find the poles to get my tent up that I realised there had been no other visitors to this bar on a campsite a few miles off the beaten track. A fleeting concern was soon replaced by the conundrum as to whether to sleep in an unpitched tent or outside it. I chose the former which worked well with the exception of feeling like I was pasted to the wall of a sauna on awaking. This was soon to be replaced by a thumping headache which reminded me of my mothers saying that "nothing is free, even good things have a price".

Northern Germany and Poland were gloriously sunny and crossed by roads which could have doubled as aeroplane runways given their size and lack of traffic. That said a couple of detours led to getting lost late in the evening and initial panic replaced by overwhelming relief as kind passers-by took time to stop and communicate accurate directions in colourful homemade sign language.

My motorbike fell over whilst getting petrol at a station in Kanus. Within seconds I had two young guys helping me pick up everything. When it became apparent that the clutch lever had broken, they offered to get a van and bring me to a garage. Although I hadn't seen the news for a while, I was still dogged by the usual scepticism that people have an ulterior motive and declined their kind offer.

What a mistake... it took eight hours in baking temperatures (at times exceeding 40 degrees) and countless phone calls to get the bike collected and brought to a garage. I then called a taxi and was brought to a campsite close to the city centre. (Which by the way I had written off previously as too central.) But what luck... well in the end it was luck. The first night I was happy to have somewhere reasonably safe to camp and felt the bike would be repaired quickly. But numerous calls on the following day to the insurance company failed to locate the garage to which it had been brought.

Meanwhile on the second day the manager of the campsite Adomas noticed I was hanging around making phone calls and spent the afternoon contacting motorcycle repair shops but to no avail. By day three on the campsite I was trying to work out how I would get to my flight in Tallin before the end of the week. The intention had been to drive the bike to Narva in Russia and then leave it in Tallin over the winter to return the following summer to take on another adventure.

All this seemed a pipe dream by this stage until Domantas the owner of the campsite discovered my dilemma and took me under his wing. In a couple of hours he put the word out to many friends who had motorbikes and it seemed like all of Lithuania was trying to help me. Unbelievably the problem was solved before nightfall with the bike which had been left at the side of a car dealership being located and fixed.

Whilst the help of so many strangers like Pierre, Lina, Adomas and Domantas practically on a daily basis didn't cure my scepticism as it probably should, they have given me the gift of questioning it and for that I am very grateful.

Liam – the middle-aged Civil Servant.

My big event started from a very small outing. We were visiting friends of my wife (James and Lisa) in Dorchester one weekend and they asked us if we would like to go sailing for a few hours on the Saturday. I wasn't aware that they were wealthy and was pleasantly surprised at the idea of spending the afternoon on a yacht.

We met the couple at the marina and they seemed just as "normal" as I had remembered them. It was with great anticipation that I walked down the pontoon passing boats of all sizes waiting to be directed to our vessel for the day. I was slightly surprised when we were shown on to "Calmways" their boat as it was absolutely beautiful. Everything from the railings to the benches were glistening in the sun. But I was flabbergasted when told that their Nicholson 32 Long Keal boat was built in 1969 and it only cost them £18,000 to buy and completely refurbish. They outlined that they simply decided to downgrade their car so that they could have sailing in their lives. We had a wonderful afternoon and it soon became apparent that you need two things for sailing, namely brains and brawn, and you can guess what I brought to the table.

This one trip led to many more and the double bonus was that my wife was also happy in meeting Lisa regularly.

After about a year of fun on the weekends James asked if I would like to sail around Britain. At first it sounded like a great idea as James mentioned all the lovely places we could call to which I had only heard of before, like Wick at the top of Scotland to Douglas in the Isle of Man. But then it transpired that it would take two months which I simply couldn't afford from a work perspective.

I had thought no more of it until James phoned me one evening with a revised idea. Why not take the holiday elemet out of the trip and "instead work our butts off" to circumnavigate Britain in a month on a 50-year-old boat raising money for charity? In an instant all the hurdles vanished. I never like spending time away from family but creating a major fundraising initiative to support those in need balanced my outlook. In addition, I knew a month away from work would be tricky but manageable and again I could probably justify it to myself if for a good cause.

What followed that summer was possibly the toughest and most invigorating month of my life. After leaving Weymouth we went clockwise. Rounding Lands End was scary as the seas were high but was only a taster of what we had in store. It was to be the start of an emotional rollercoaster ride. I have never been more afraid than when we got caught in a storm off the Bristol Channel nor more contented when sailing on what seemed like sheer glass off Filey Brigg in North

Yorkshire.

The winds got to force 10 off Bristol and we would have been worried but ok, except that a pin came out of the forward port stay (holding the mast in place) and it started swinging free. Ultimately this meant that the mast could come down at any minute with implications ranging from injuring myself or James to putting a hole in the boat and causing us to sink. We had no other option but to double tether ourselves to the boat and go up front in the rolling waves to replace the pin. In truth it was almost a surprise that we managed to replace the pin without one of us getting washed overboard. They say everything is relative and as crazy as it seems we actually relaxed once we knew the mast was safe even though we had to deal with force 10 winds for another three hours.

Apart from the storm we were unlucky on a number of occasions like when our inflatable boat deflated whilst rowing to shore for provisions in Portree Harbour on the Isle of Sky but we were very lucky on many more such as getting safely into port out of a fog in Stonehaven or when a ship narrowly missed us in the Humber Estuary.

We overnighted at both Douglas and Wick but what I gained from the adventure was much more than ticking boxes or increasing my knowledge about sailing but learning about myself. I now know I can achieve both mentally and physically much more than I ever believed but that the price of being brave and strong is the experience of overcoming periods when feeling afraid and weak.

Mary – the young solicitor with an image to keep.
A couple of years ago my father passed away and it possibly had a greater impact on my life than any other event to date. For the first time I realised that we are all travelling along the same very short road of life with no

way of turning back. I thought the feeling was part of the grieving process and would pass with time but it hasn't. Instead it's like the last gift I received from my Dad which helps me to embrace life and not to waste time worrying about the small stuff.

It was this frame of mind that helped me convince my friend from college, Sarah, to retrace the interrail trip we had taken twenty years ago around Europe. To relieve the guilt of using family money we decided that we would adopt a frugal approach by staying in hostels and eating cheaply. Our route was Paris, Amsterdam, Frankfurt, Zurich, Milan, Barcelona, Paris and home. Whilst we had completed the trip in just over three weeks on the first occasion my life has changed a little (tongue in cheek) and between work and home could only manage two weeks.

Nothing can replace the feeling of being young but once we pass those few fleeting teenage years of wishing the opposite most of us spend varying degrees of time and money trying to recapture it. As I stood looking up at the departure times in London St. Pancras twenty years vanished. For a brief second, I was transported back in time to a world where my parents were young and healthy, and worries revolved around my latest crush rather than the daily rush of family life. For that moment alone the whole trip was worth it.

There were many other highlights. The Louvre in Paris with its wonderful sculptures and paintings left me with a sense of wonder that I didn't experience on the first occasion. I am not sure if the feeling related to an appreciation of the beauty of the individual works of art or to my having ten minutes to do nothing but calmly admire the painting. It dawned on me that perhaps that is what the artist may have really wanted; not to have their painting criticised for lack of light or sculpture for dimensional flaws but to take the viewer to a serene place in their own mind where beauty consists of contentment rather than anything the eye can behold.

Amsterdam was the postcard I remembered with its many canals surrounded by wonderful building facades only comparable to dolls houses. Their liberal views and adoption of cycling in all weathers seems to create more than an environmentally friendly and efficient mode of transport. In contrast to many cities where the daily toll of life seems to be etched on the faces of the inhabitants in Amsterdam cycling in this wonderful environment seems to invigorate rather than debilitate daily life. I have a wonderful image in my mind of an older lady cycling in a classical dress and beautiful makeup who in the brief moment of passing me gave off the aura of a young lady on the cusp of life.

Each city brought its own highlights which have been better described by those more eloquent than I. Although we did have our Thelma and Louise like moment in Milan which is better left in the folklore of Italian night life.   The highlight was very much contrary to my expectations and my recollection of twenty years previously in that it related to the joy we gained from staying in hostels. Deep uninhibited conversations with young strangers reminded me of who I am and what is key to me in life. That having fun is more important than a new car and being truly available for friends and family is more important than the next promotion. I rediscovered we need to connect with other people to be happy.

They say travel broadens the mind and feeds the soul, but I think this has less to do with the places visited and more with the people encountered. I am thankful to my Dad for giving me the motivation to get out there and discover this again.

Printed in Great Britain
by Amazon

65799494R00087